Thinking on Housing

If we do stop to think on housing, what do we see? What is housing and what does it do? These seem deceptively simple questions, but they are often left unanswered. The reason for this is that a lot of discourse on housing is really a concern for policy-making and the critical evaluation of existing policies. Discourse, is not, properly speaking, on housing at all. It is concerned with provision, distribution and access, but this thinking on housing stops at the front door. It is only concerned with what is actually external to housing.

But for most people, housing already exists and they have access to it. Housing is not then about policy, but about how we can use what is a complex object in a manner that allows us to live well. Housing, for most of us, is about what we do when the front door is firmly shut and we are free from the external world.

These essays explore this idea of housing as an object that exists for use. Housing is pictured as an object that contains activity. These pieces look at what we do with housing once we have it and so provides a necessary underpinning for any understanding of why housing is important.

A further purpose of these pieces is to present different ways of thinking and writing on housing. It is an attempt to show that housing is a suitable topic for philosophical discourse. It is suggested that we can and should seek to establish a philosophy of housing, rather than just relying on the traditional social sciences.

Peter King is a writer and thinker on housing issues. He has consistently used philosophical concepts to draw out the meaning of housing. He is the author of 20 books including *A Social Philosophy of Housing* (Ashgate, 2003), *Private Dwelling* (Routledge, 2004) and *The Principles of Housing* (Routledge, 2016). Peter is currently Reader in Social Thought at De Montfort University.

Routledge Focus: Housing and Philosophy

Routledge Focus offers both established and early-career academics the flexibility to publish cutting-edge commentary on topical issues, policy-focused research, analytical or theoretical innovations, in-depth case studies, or short topics for specialized audiences. The format and speed to market is distinctive. Routledge Focus books are 20,000 to 50,000 words and will be published as eBooks and in Hardback as print on demand.

This series seeks to develop the links between housing and philosophy. It seeks proposals from academics and policy makers on any aspect of philosophy and its relation to housing. This might include ethics, political and social philosophy, and aesthetics, as well as logic, epistemology and metaphysics. All proposals are expected to apply philosophical rigour to the exploration of housing phenomena, whether this be the policy making process, design, or the manner in which individuals and communities relate to housing. The series seeks an international and comparative focus and is particularly keen to include innovative and distinctly new approaches to the study of housing.

Please contact Peter King (pjking@dmu.ac.uk) with ideas for book proposals or for further details.

Books in the series:

Peter King, *Thinking on Housing: Words, Memories, Use*

Thinking on Housing
Words, Memories, Use

Peter King

Routledge
Taylor & Francis Group

LONDON AND NEW YORK

First published 2017 by Routledge

2 Park Square, Milton Park, Abingdon, Oxon OX14 4RN
605 Third Avenue, New York, NY 10017

Routledge is an imprint of the Taylor & Francis Group, an informa business

First issued in paperback 2021

British Library Cataloguing-in-Publication Data
A catalogue record for this book is available from the British Library

Library of Congress Cataloging-in-Publication Data
A catalog record for this book has been requested

ISBN: 978-1-138-29384-7 (hbk)
ISBN: 978-1-03-217922-3 (pbk)
DOI: 10.4324/9781315231846

Typeset in Sabon
by Apex CoVantage, LLC

To B, H and R
For being there and letting me be theirs

Contents

Preface

This is a book on how we think, and then come to talk, on housing. Housing, I wish to suggest, is the *only thing*. Housing is a thing in itself, substantial and capable of standing on its own. We should see housing for what it is, from within, and without any preconceived shape determined by things outside of housing. We do not wish housing to be accommodated within a space already created for another purpose.

It is the focus, the very purpose, and it is not subsidiary to anything bigger. Housing does not need to be propped up by anything else. It already has its own foundations. We do not need to take any pre-existing theory or off-the-shelf concept and use it to underpin housing. Housing does not need to be plugged into anything else to give it meaning. Housing can stand alone.

What we are not doing is referring to the manner in which 'housing' is used most frequently, where there is another word coupled to it but most often left unsaid. This word is 'policy'. Many, when they speak of housing, are in actual fact referring to 'housing policy'. They are not really talking about housing, but are concerned rather with the policies that make and maintain housing. These discussions, properly speaking, are not really about housing at all, but are about a concern for the actions of institutions and agents that lead to the development, management, maintenance and financing of housing. It is a concern for the provision of housing and the standards that govern this provision.[1]

Now while policy discourse has its place, it also has a major fault: it takes housing as a given that needs no further explanation. The role of policy stops at the front door, and so to be concerned with policy is to show an interest in making dwellings but not in how they are used. It

1 King (1996).

is akin to being interested in how cars are made but not in seeing them as a mode of transport. But car manufacture is not an end in itself, and we do not build houses in order to have policies or be playthings for policy-makers. We have houses so that we can use them to maintain ourselves and fulfil our ends.

The key to understanding housing is our day-to-day use of it, which needs no direct intervention from outside of the housing itself. Nor do we need to deliberate on it for it to work for us. It is not something that has to be set up as an event. To make housing into a specific event is to separate it from its basic use. Likewise, we neither need policies, nor have to recognise the role of the policy-maker, in order to have housing that works. Indeed, when housing works we can happily shut the door on policy.

So we should return to housing as a thing in itself; as something that is elemental and not derivative. Housing depends on nothing but those who make it and use it. Housing has its own essence, and the purpose of research should be to discover this, to describe it and make it known. We need to define housing and defend it on these same terms.

Accordingly, we should avoid the temptation of diluting housing through integration into pre-existing theoretical structures that serve only to relegate housing to a subservient status. What we similarly need to avoid is the idea that housing is merely a case study to elucidate a particular theory. Education is considered substantial enough to be a field in itself, with its own concepts, and so are medicine and agriculture. All of these, like housing, derive from practice, and as fields of study they are abstractions out of practice. They derive from a set of empirical conditions and from these have come core concepts that in turn provide us with a structure of understanding that can stand without external support. Social theories become additive to these concepts and structure, rather than essential or definitive. So, with housing, we can suggest that theories might link into housing but they cannot make it, and to attempt to make housing out of pre-existing theories is to diminish it as subsidiary. We need to avoid simply seeing housing as the case study to illustrate a theory, as if it is the latter that is the real substance.

Instead of approaching housing from pre-established concepts, theories and methodologies, we should take housing on its own terms. Some fields of enquiry require technical knowledge, experience and a high level of judgement, as in the case of medicine. Medicine has developed its own modes of discourse based on practice. Those of us looking at housing should be aiming to do precisely the same: to develop housing as a body of procedures that derive from practice.

This is not to put housing in the same category as medicine. Housing lacks the same level of technical knowledge and need for judgement as medicine, being reliant more on experience and use, of activities at the level of organisations, professionals and households. It is the latter – households – that create the major epistemological differences from medicine, in that the views of the users need not be mediated by professionals in anything like the same way. This means we can come to housing in a distinct and direct manner when we try to conceptualise it. Housing is much more transparent in the epistemic sense, in that it is open to all and not just those with expertise and judgement, and so we cannot limit access to it in the same way as entry into a profession is limited.[2] Housing is not really about expertise at all, but about connections and an appreciation of the nature of use. Yet, by close observation of the use of housing we can describe it.

Indeed, the aim here is to describe housing itself and not to overlay it with any construction that detracts from housing in itself. This necessitates a rigorous descriptive method based on housing as it is.

What we wish to discuss are the elementals of housing. These are the things that make housing what it is and which then allow everything else to stand upon it. Much of what we call housing is relatively stable and does not change, even as we act as if the very opposite is true. We tend to lose sight of this stability by focusing instead on small innovations and policy developments, which enrapture us for a time before we turn to the next fad. With each fad we maintain our enthusiasm, hoping not to be caught out by the latest thing, not be seen as cynical, divisive, naïve or old fashioned. The fact that these little innovations follow each other so quickly presents the illusion of constant change, and the impression that we have to be constantly running to keep up. However, the real basis of housing remains unchanged. The manner in which it can be used has not altered.

The basis of these fads is often not substantial but is really focused on a change in terminology. It seems that through the redesignation of a concept or a policy we can actually suggest it is new and innovative. Hence the change in terminology with regard to subsidised housing in the UK, from 'council housing' to 'social housing' to 'affordable housing', which shifts the focus from how the dwellings are owned to why they exist and who they are let to, and then on to a moralising sense of purpose. These new terms take on a specific meaning that then separates them from ordinary language and helps speakers

2 King (2003).

defend themselves from the apparently naïve. Thus questions of why anyone would be stupid enough to build housing that is not affordable, or why housing that is deemed to be unaffordable is sustainably occupied, are ignored in favour of an apparently sophisticated belief that we have got to the heart of the problem. Yet, in all too short a period of time, the terminology will shift again and those caught out using an old-fashioned term will be looked down upon. However, the essence of the housing problem that necessitated the building of council housing in the past and affordable housing now has not changed. Perhaps the need for constant change in terminology is necessary precisely because of the failure of past policies to meet their intended aims, and so giving existing entities new names helps us to forget past failures while renewing in us the hope that we are not wasting our time rushing around.

One result of this churning of concepts is a constant inflation of what housing contains. The idea of housing continually grows to encompass new priorities, intentions and connections, but always without jettisoning what had gone before. So housing appears to become ever more complex as it changes seemingly constantly, leaving us struggling to comprehend what is actually going on. But much of this complexity is invented, seemingly necessary because complexity gives an impression of significance and sophistication.

§

These essays need not be read as a whole, and they are written in different styles, from the playful to the highly abstract. But they all see housing in the same way. Housing is not embedded in anything else but is a thing in itself. To restate our point of departure, housing is the only thing. It is the sole focus of our thinking. Housing is not an adjunct or something we use to qualify another discourse: there is nothing that needs to be added onto the word 'housing' to make it substantial enough for serious consideration. Housing, for us, is all there is. Once we, as thinkers on housing, have this straight, we might get somewhere.

This book is an exercise in thinking speculatively on housing. The ideas presented here have their antecedents, but the book is intended primarily as an attempt to break away from existing ways of thinking and writing about housing. Many thinkers have influenced me over the past 30 years. In particular, my debts to Gaston Bachelard, Martin Heidegger and John Turner will be all too apparent in what follows. But also running under my thinking in a rather less obvious way is Emanuel Swedenborg's doctrine of use. Many of the influences on these essays, however, have been implicit, in that the genesis of the current work was to return to a number of my previous books and consciously rework a number of the concepts I had developed. The result is a very condensed presentation of what I take housing to consist of. My aim has been to bring these concepts together into a coherent whole. Rather than clog up the text with references I have taken the liberty of writing a brief note at the end of this book that details the main sources for each of the chapters. However, where appropriate I have provided footnotes to reference sources directly quoted in the text.

What I have tried to achieve is a form of thinking on housing that can be expressed in a different manner from traditional academic discourse. I want to get away from the embedded nature of this discourse, with its reliance on a certain literature and a particular argumentative style. This is not entirely, I hope, out of some gratuitous desire to be different or wilful. Rather, what I have sought to do is to think on housing in a manner that is direct and unmediated. What I am trying to do is to portray housing as naked and new. I have used sources that help me do this, and have deliberately avoided the traditional literature for fear that it would tie me back into the old forms of thinking.

If we are looking at housing differently, then perhaps we need a distinct vocabulary and means of expression. Is it really possible to say what we wish to say using the conventional language of housing policy discourse with its already ingrained meanings? Might we not need to develop new concepts and categories that suit this new purpose? To do this we need to look at housing in a distinctly different manner, using approaches beyond the social sciences. It may also involve pulling apart conventional concepts and rebuilding them in a distinct way, or it may be a matter of using new and distinct terms and fighting to establish their meaning and intent as part of a new housing discourse. In essence, what I am doing is constructing a new form of discourse rather than writing in the traditional academic manner. I have largely relied on what might be termed an intuitive approach that is based on introspection rather than empirical analysis. It seems to me that housing, with its reliance on the subjective and the intimate, is ripe for the sorts of speculation that a certain form of introspective thinking can offer. This intuitive approach, which relies on building up concepts from the actual practice of housing, has tremendous potential for developing a housing discourse that is much closer to the users and which does not rely on concepts from outside of housing.

In case it is not already obvious, I have no pretensions to call this a scientific approach, nor do I see this as in any way problematical. I see nothing wrong with taking an apparently 'unscientific' approach to something as personal and subjective as housing. Indeed, to my mind, the attempt to treat housing in a purportedly scientific manner is at the root of much of what is wrong with housing discourse, particularly the inability to focus on housing as the only thing.

I have always tried to approach housing philosophically. I have consistently used philosophical concepts and methods to try to understand housing. But using philosophical concepts is not the same as *doing* philosophy. One can apply philosophy to housing, as I have done frequently, but this does not mean that one is creating a philosophy of housing, nor does it imply that this is either necessary or possible. Interestingly, a web search of 'housing philosophy' reveals a series of links to US universities that talk about their 'housing philosophy', by which they mean the approach they have to housing their students. What they are referring to here are the principles by which they conduct their accommodation service. Indeed, we might suggest that they are using the word 'philosophy' precisely to suggest that they have a principled approach. But they are not, of course, looking at housing philosophically.

We can show the distinction by replacing 'housing' with 'religion'. There is a ready and obvious distinction between 'philosophy of religion' and 'religious philosophy'. The former is the philosophical study of religions, while the latter is a particular approach towards religion that may be based on certain distinct principles but which need not be anything to do with a philosophical method.[3]

Returning to housing, we might say then that 'philosophy of housing' suggests we are looking at housing in a particular manner and using distinct concepts and methods, whereas 'housing philosophy' might just relate to a particular approach to housing people. It ought to be clear that what I am attempting here is 'philosophy of'.

But with so much wrong with the world, including homelessness, inequality and poverty, how can this be justified? Are there not much more pressing questions than the abstractions presented here? The first answer to this question is to state that what is being attempted here can do no harm. Academic discourse has only ever a limited effect and most noticeably affects only other academics, so writing this will make nothing worse than it already is. This may be a minimum condition, but it is one to hold onto. Second, there is already a considerable

---

3 I know that using the word 'religious' means we are using a noun now as an adverb, but we can do this too with the word 'housing' without its form changing, as in 'housing association'.

body of work on policy issues, but no one is really attempting to do what is contained here. Third, and related to the two previous points, this current work should be seen as additional to what has been done before and to what others are currently doing. This work takes nothing away from anyone else, nor does it prevent others from focusing on any other issues they wish to. Fourth, and to be positive, we might actually state that understanding the 'what' and 'why' of things is thoroughly important. It might actually help us avoid future problems and explain why current problems are as they are. An unreflective approach to housing, even one driven by a sense of necessity, might not produce the outcomes we wish and might even cause more harm than good. So a little more reflection might actually help prevent mistakes in the first place.

The purpose of this book, then, is to think differently on housing, and consequently to also talk on it in a distinct manner. It seeks to question the way in which housing discourse is often conducted and, through a rather different mode of discourse, cause some people to think again.

Chapter 1
Thinking on housing

This book seeks to provide a spotlight on housing. What we are doing here is thinking *on* housing and not thinking *about* it. This is the difference between a spotlight and a floodlight. A spotlight is targeted *on* something specific. It is a bright light shining on a small area. It highlights something and makes it the sole focus of attention, whereas a floodlight gives a more diffuse and general light. A floodlight literally floods an area with light. It is less specific, less targeted and aimed at a more general coverage.

To think on housing is to see housing as the only thing, the sole focus of our studies. We are concerned with housing and nothing else. 'Thinking about' is more general and implies we are looking at housing and the things around it, on the connections and things nearby. But we want here to focus only on one thing and to highlight it and understand it fully, and to do this before we start to make connections and linkages. There is a need to put a narrow spotlight on housing, to give it star billing, and to keep everything else for the moment in darkness. The thinking needs to be *on* housing and not around and about it. There needs to be a direct focus that is singular rather than a diffuse lack of focus whereby we might be attracted by something outside of housing and allow it to dominate our thoughts at the expense of the one thing that really matters.

What does thinking on housing involve? It is the undertaking of the rigorous examination of concepts, ideas and initiatives on housing. It is not restricted to any particular method or approach, nor is it linked to any particular discipline. We are not claiming any scientific status for our endeavours here. Indeed, this is a crucial point. There is no particular disciplinary focus. Instead there is simply a focus on the subject of housing – it is thinking on housing and only housing. We are placing housing at the centre: it is housing we are looking at and not discipline-based methods and theories. We are, so to speak, being housing-centric.

We are concerned with taking housing discourse further than it has currently gone. We are not seeking to apply existing disciplinary frameworks to housing without expecting housing to change in the process. What we are doing is not passive. We expect housing to be active and for discourse to develop in new ways and form new patterns as we open up what housing is and does more fully. Thinking on housing therefore does not rely on existing concepts, theories or methods but rather focuses critically on housing as the only thing.

So there is no attempt to build a theory or to model housing in any way. There is no attempt to build a system. We are looking to develop concepts and ideas that come out of housing rather than attempt to bolt housing onto any already existing conceptual apparatus. Thinking need not be strictly theoretical, therefore, but rather requires the application of rigorous analysis to housing. What we wish to do instead is to describe housing in its generality. By this we mean housing as an object of interaction, as a receptacle, as background and as a flow. Housing can be seen as an object of activity. Housing is an object that has an activity as its intrinsic quality. Housing *holds*: it bears use and meaning.

The worth of these thoughts is in the light they throw onto housing, and that is all. As thoughts they are self-contained and have no absolute purpose beyond themselves. They are only on housing and attempt to say nothing beyond housing. They are neither first thoughts nor last thoughts.

The clarity or obscurity of these thoughts is a function of the capability of thinking in this manner. We have moved to another place and rely on rather different foundations for our thinking. But this is thinking that needs to be done. There is a current lack of clarity, with the seriousness of housing hidden under a cloak of policy discourse and the traces of disciplines that bring already formed abstractions to bear on housing. But in doing so, they leave obfuscatory layers of preconception over housing that prevents thinking that is clear and precisely targeted.

The aim of the thinking here on housing is both to isolate it and to keep it in its place. We must not move it, progress it or persuade it to join with others. We must not misname it or confuse it with what it is not. We must not lose it in a mangled mess of otherwise unconnected thoughts. We are only interested in housing.

This thinking is not concerned with its reaction to other things. We do not wish to compare, to relativise or to make unnecessary associations. We do not wish to embed our thoughts in anything other than housing. This is thinking as a description of things as we see them.

Thinking, however, has consequences. Thoughts are definitive: they may end nothing or they may keep on, but once stated, thoughts are there and they are capable. All thought builds on what has been thought already, but it can also start new things. Thoughts can be beginnings, the spark that lights the fires of invention. Thinking is an attempt at understanding, but with no necessity of being final, of finding a solution. Once stated, a thought remains present, to be added to, criticised, contradicted or ignored. The intention of a thought need not be accepted, but nor should it necessarily be ignored. We should not impute motive but instead simply reflect on what has been thought and said.

This discourse on housing most assuredly has its limitations. Principally, it assumes that housing already exists. We have little concern here for supply, affordability or access. We are solely concerned with how we can use what already exists. We are not suggesting that supply and affordability are unimportant, but merely that a discourse based on these things tends to obscure a discourse of equal significance. We are suggesting something additional to existing topics of housing discourse and not trying to supplant them. We are not trying to advocate this approach as the only one, or argue that it should be pursued to the exclusion of anything else. Rather, we wish to pursue this approach because of its apparent utility.

Perhaps a more fundamental limitation has already been alluded to: that the intensity of thinking on housing is completely at odds with the thing itself and our use of it. Thinking on housing prevents complacency and stops us using it in its unconscious completeness. There is a price to pay for thinking in this way, and that is in the leisure to enjoy our own use of housing as a non-reflective object.

Like housing, a term which encompasses both the unaffordable commodity and the loose doorknob, thinking moves from the consequential to the banal and back again, and with little awareness of the consequences of what really matters. But sooner or later, thinking on housing always returns us to what we are doing just now, and in *this place*. Because to think seriously on housing is to focus on what it is to become located, to be placed, to be pinned in position, and for us to recognise that this locatedness is what really matters in making housing the place which, sooner or later, we must always return to.

But housing is not home, and in our thinking we should clearly distinguish between the two. This is because 'home' is no longer a term we can use with any certainty or much comfort. It has been captured by policy to refer simply to units of accommodation, to mere brick boxes. Developers build 'homes', social landlords manage 'homes' and governments boast about how many 'homes' they have funded. What matters here is that the word used is now always 'homes': it is a plural, a collection of entities that become anonymous by their amalgamation into the whole. This use has led to a cheapening of the concept of home, reducing it to a sentimentalised vehicle for aspiration. 'Housing', on the other hand, is much more than home. It is a much bigger concept. Housing connects us with the full range of meaningful use. 'Home' is merely used as a noun, while 'housing' can be, and is, both noun and verb. Housing connects us to things and to actions. There is no ambiguity. We use housing, but what does it mean to use home now that it has been so adulterated by the language of policy? When we talk of meaning – as we must – we refer to housing and know this to be more extensive than home. Housing is an activity without the limits of home. It can take us outside and allows us to touch the implacability of the object that is the house without compromise. Housing is outside and inside; it is not just façade, even though we need the face to be there. Home lacks a façade other than providing cover for sentimentality.

Housing contains the past, the present and the future. It is what we are currently doing and what we have now. But it is also what we did and had before, and what we may do and have in a time to come. Housing is both a store of memory and is stored in memory. Housing is for the future, for what might yet be. It can carry our hopes, even as they might be deluded. Housing is what we had then, have now and might still have.

We can object to housing but not to home. We can object to policy and aspiration, and housing allows us to do so. Policy and aspiration only pervert home while they keep housing intact. Home is used precisely because it can only be positive, and so it sentimentalises aspiration as a utopian future.

If these studies of thinking on housing have one over-riding strength, it is that they actually inform us as to why all other studies, be they on supply, affordability or access, are important. They form a necessary propaedeutic to policy studies on housing. They are not merely an alternative, but a crucial underpinning for more conventional studies. These studies do not answer all of the important questions, but they do answer the *most* important: *what does housing do?*

The need for this approach to housing can be justified in three basic statements. First, much of the existing literature that purports to discuss housing is simply a concern with policy and policy-making. Second, *policy is not housing*, as it cannot explain the gathering of meaning through use. Third, housing is important precisely and entirely because of how we use it and what meanings we come to attach to it as a result.

This work is essentially a commentary and development of these three statements. The chapters that follow explore a series of concepts that substantiate these statements. They do not prove them, because this is not our aim. They do not say that they are the only things that matter about housing. However, they will help in our appreciation of housing as the only thing.

Much of what we have to say about housing makes the saying redundant, but only after it has been said. Housing only appears as it really is in a certain light, and only then to those who know how to look. By this we mean that we have to think about housing in the right way. Once we are able to achieve this we will then appreciate that the significance of housing is precisely in its ability to *lose* significance. We will then have the ability to use housing, and use it well, without even attempting to understand the role that housing plays and why it does work well.

Chapter 2
Housing is

We can say what 'housing' is and we can try to provide a tight definition. It is a noun that describes a collection of physical structures capable of allowing human residence. It is a verb that describes the activity of providing, managing and maintaining that collection of physical structures. But once we have done that, what then? What does this actually tell us? We can say what a house is; we can measure it and value it and we can compare it with other dwellings. But what does this really tell us? How far does this really go towards explaining the significance of housing?

Housing may be the only thing – the focus of our attention – but, properly speaking, it is made up of many things and it connects us to many more. There is no contradiction here, in saying that housing is both the only thing and that it is made up of many things, because there are many things that come out of – derive from – housing. Housing is not an accessory, an adjunct, a subsidiary or a peripheral. Housing is the thing that encloses us along with all those other things that matter to us. Housing allows us to keep things close. We are enclosed by housing, and it encloses all we are, all we have and even all we might wish to be. We make much of our housing, as a nest, as a refuge, as a home. But it is still more than this. It is through being enclosed by housing that we are able to weave a meaningful life for ourselves. It is how we are able to bring distinct things together. The enclosure that is housing allows us to settle with things that we need and wish to use.

Housing is where we include things that become meaningful by this enclosed inclusion. We might say then that housing is inclusive because it is capable of enclosing. But being enclosed, these things are not in plain sight. We cannot, as an observer, a researcher, a thinker on housing, come to see these things directly. We have, of course, our own experiences as dwellers within housing, and we have our knowledge of family and friends and what we can glean from our popular culture of how others live. But the very enclosure of housing prevents us from seeing in too far, and so we have to be indirect and come at housing from a different path. Instead of the direct path of definitions and clear descriptions, we have to come to housing via a winding path, picking up clues and signs about what direction we should move in. In other words, instead of housing *is*, we can only know housing *as*. We can know housing only through allusion and association. Even as we see housing as the only thing, we have to accept it as a bundle of things and try to disclose what these are and what they mean. We can never do this directly.

But how do we unbundle the collection of things that housing is? We can make a list and this will doubtless be helpful. But we might also look at the word 'housing' and start to play with it. We have tried to define this word, to say what it means. But what precisely does it allude to? What do we mean when we say 'housing as'? In other words (and what else have we to play with?), what can we make of the word 'housing'?

Enrique Enriquez is a Venezuelan tarot reader living in New York.[1] The very mention of tarot might raise suspicions of fortune telling, divination and the occult. It might strike others as nonsense or meaningless drivel. But Enriquez does not tell fortunes or predict the future. He is in reality a poet who is able to make pictures out of words and words out of the pictures on tarot cards, amongst other things. Enriquez finds patterns in things. He sees connections and links between things that appear to be totally disconnected, and these may help us to find some meaning in our lives. But there is meaning only because we can see the connections, either by ourselves or because they have been pointed out to us. The connections exist because of the process of pointing and showing, and then only because we recognise and accept them. Enriquez' method, then, is like the manner in which we find things, accept them and keep them close. It mirrors the manner in which we find patterns through the enclosure of housing.

In his book *Tarology*,[2] Enriquez suggests that the particular tradition of the Marseilles tarot, with its associations to the so-called language of the birds – *la langue des oiseaux* – is a 'true "science of circumstance", where iconographically irrelevant details acquire a

---

1 Perhaps the best way to discover Enriquez is through the film *Tarology* (directed by Chris Deleo, 2013), which shows him in action, particularly how he paints pictures out of words.

2 Enriquez (2011).

fundamental importance and everything we see is taken to be part of a bigger, albeit non verifiable scheme'.[3] This, according to Enriquez, is a matter not of revealing meaning but creating it. There are no hidden messages secreted within a text, 'rather we are creating new meanings that weren't necessarily implicit in the original text'.[4] This is an exercise in pattern recognition and, accordingly, one in which we will tend to find what we are looking for, 'unless we aren't looking for anything, in which case we may just enjoy the surprises the words contain'.[5]

What we are doing then is literally playing with words. We take certain words that are important to us – 'house' and 'housing' – and we break them up into their component elements – letters – and recombine them to create meanings that we can associate with the original word. These new words depend upon our understanding of the original word, but also take us further and create associations beyond the everyday sense of the term. It is not a scientific approach, nor is it intended to be. It is playful and pataphysical,[6] using words and letters to throw up allusions. These allusions might surprise us, they might delight us and they might make us think. There is no explicit purpose to it – unless, of course, anyone chooses to see a purpose, and then there is one.

What we have here is a process that is truly subversive of positivism. Many academics claim to eschew positivism, but they do so only at the margins. They question total answers and the reductive nature of conventional science. They apply approaches that deconstruct, subvert or fracture the positivistic nature of science. Yet they still wish to remain within the general remit of science. They still depend on rational and logical processes. They present an argument; they try to demolish the arguments of others; they try to prove their case and supplant that of others. In this sense they are using only an attenuated positivist approach. They, too, depend on the rationales of positivism to make themselves understood and gain acceptance.

Enriquez's pataphysical approach eschews any notion of science and assumes that whatever meaning and sense can be gleaned from these descriptions will be indirect and allusive. There are no proofs, no conclusions. All we have are associations.

We are interested not just in words but in their component parts, the letters that make up words. Enriquez suggests that we can see the

3 Ibid., pp. 67–8.
4 Ibid., p. 75.
5 Op. cit.
6 See Hughill (2012).

consonants of a word as the body and the vowels as the soul. The vowels are made by opening the throat and are made by open breath, but the consonants are made by restricting the breath, by putting a structure in place to stop it and to hold it back. Consonants are obstacles we put in front of the air coming into our throats that modify the vowels to make sounds we understand as words.

We can show associations by looking at the letters themselves – certain letters present us with meanings iconographically, because of their shape and form. Thus the body of the word 'HOUSE' is 'HS' (using capital letters). The shape of the letters links to snakes and ladders and the idea of rushing up the ladder or down the snake; of good fortune or bad luck, or making the most of an opportunity and then losing it all. This is like the property market where housing is reduced to assets. Housing becomes nothing but a game, a race to the top with winners and losers. It reminds us that what goes up can also go down. Indeed, we need to go up – we need the boom – before we can fall and go bust. We have the bust only because of the preceding boom, and these go together like snakes and ladders. So we are impelled to see housing as an asset that leads us into a game that we might find hard to control, and where there are as many losers as winners.

The soul of 'HOUSE' is 'OUE', and this sounds like 'owe' or 'ow'. We end up owing a lot of money in order to buy our asset, and this might lead to an exclamation of pain. When we ride the boom we feel good, but when the bust comes so does the pain, and we cannot help but feel it. And we are still left owing for an asset that has deluded us.

But all is not gloom: the letter 'O' reminds us of the whole, of the world where everything is connected. It is also enclosed, providing a secure boundary in which we can thrive. The letter 'U' is like a cup, a receptacle that holds things which otherwise would be shapeless and amorphous, just as we would if we lacked a place to live. But the cup – the 'U' – is looking up, it is open to the heavens and so can be seen as positive and open to aspiration and hope. But because of its shape it is static and not active: 'U' can sustain its position and so it can keep things contained.

'E' can be taken to be everything. It contains the three levels of the physical, the emotional and the intellectual. It shows us that the house contains all and is not merely a place of shelter. But 'E' is also reaching out: its three arms are literally reaching towards its neighbour. It is expanding to become inclusive and accepting of all. With letters rearranged, 'house' contains both 'she' and 'he'. It gives us an identity and tells us who we are. But 'he' is within 'she', which is within 'house', so we can be as ambiguous with our identity as we choose. From house we can also get 'use', which is the very element of what the house is, a place that we can use, where we can be 'she' or 'he' and be there together as 'us'. House leads to 'shoe', a thing that we hope fits us well, that is comfortable and that we can use continually throughout the day. It gives us 'hoe', a tool that we can use to manage what is around us. Our house too is a tool, something that we can use to further our ends. The word 'sue' reminds us that we have to pay for our house . . . or else. It can be a place that causes us to be complacent and to forget that others matter – 'So?' – and a cause of uncertainty and misunderstanding – 'Eh?' and 'Uh?' – or of surprise – 'Oh!'

But we can extend this by collectivising 'house' to make 'HOUSING'. The body of the word is similar to house – HSNG – and we can make the same reference to snakes and ladders and all that means. The letter 'N' has a sense of one leaning against another, as if for support, just as we rely on the structure of the dwelling. The letter 'G' is a circle not quite closed, and so it shows that we can escape and things can enter: we can never be completely secure. But the letter 'G' also looks like a grasping hand and this connects us with the idea of possession, of again climbing the ladder to gain as much as we can. The soul of 'HOUSING' is 'OUI', which we cannot ignore is French for 'yes'. Again it presents the connected and enclosed world with 'O' (but qualified by the 'G') and the open-topped and welcoming 'U'. It also now includes the letter 'I', which reminds us of the individual and that housing allows us to choose, to be ourselves and to be separate from others. 'I' is upright and freestanding, showing independence and freedom from others.

The word 'housing' does not quite include 'house'. It is most of the word, but not all. There is no inclusive 'E'. What should this tell us? That it is not complete and that there is something missing when we use 'housing'? That something has been lost in the extension from the one to the many? Perhaps there is a clue in that it also does not allow us to make the word 'use'. Housing collectivises and standardises 'house' and turns it into something that is necessarily impersonal. The word 'housing', we should note, does not allow for either 'he' or 'she', even if we can find the word 'son'.

But there is much that 'housing' does include and enclose. It contains the word 'sun' and we can see housing as life-giving and sustaining: it is an existential necessity. We make 'hug' to show the need for intimacy, and 'hog' to denote the possessiveness that goes with 'I'. So perhaps we can see 'housing' as having the personal touch after all. We might 'gush' about the virtues of where we live, or perhaps how much it is now worth. It encourages the 'sin' of pride as we boast how much we think we are worth. From 'housing' we can make 'gun' – a thing that we might think can keep us safe, but which is dangerous if we use it in a certain manner. Housing can be a weapon if we misuse it and don't understand what it can do. We can find 'hi', meaning the informal welcome, but we can also get 'no', meaning we are to keep out. We only wish those that are already 'in' to be included. It is a place that tells something about 'us', that offers a 'sign' to others. We might 'sing' a 'song' of praise to our house, and once the song is 'sung' we can then 'sigh' as we relax within our enclosed and 'snug' space. Our housing works for us and it goes 'on' and on, 'un'less it stops working and then we notice it in all its complexity. Sometimes we have to 'go' out, and if we split up then we might not be able to return.

All of this is common to what we know of 'house' and 'housing'. The words and letters are *of* these words – they are literally coming out of 'house' and 'housing' – and accordingly they can point to certain ideas and meanings. These connections are not necessary, but they point to things that we know housing does. These associations are what 'house' means to us, and we can create them through a play on the very word.

But does this matter, or is this not just too flippant? Does it help to build any new houses? No, of course it does not. It does not add to the housing stock. It might not make anyone materially better off.

All this playing with words matters only if we want it to; if we choose to read it and to enjoy what we find there, then it is worthwhile. If not, then go elsewhere and occupy yourself in other ways. But do so with the understanding that what is useful is only so because we take it to be. As Enriquez states: 'If making connections proves something, it is that we can make connections. Nothing more, nothing less. Even so, in the midst of such connections we can arrive at unexpected insights'.[7] We create our meanings and see what we find, and if we can't create anything then we can always go home. There we will find in place that myriad of things that come together as housing.

7 Enriquez (2011), p. 120.

Chapter 3
Care-full use

Things matter to us because of how we are able to use them. How can things aid us to achieve our purposes? We might wish to own something out of avarice or greed, but, for most of us, most of the time, we have things because they are useful.

One particular way that we are able to show our love for others is by being useful to them. We do things for them and with them. Our lives are fulfilled when we are able to provide useful service to others, or, in other words, when we are able to care for them.

Housing is a thing that we can use. We can, most certainly, use it in any number of ways. But what housing can do that is particular to it is to facilitate our usefulness towards others by providing the enclosure necessary for care. This facility is what housing does.

Housing is not merely a brick box, or an item on a spreadsheet, or lines on a plan or a picture in an estate agent's window. We need to see housing as the containment of intimacy, use and meaning. Housing is both the object and its contents. Housing becomes the object of use and the subject of the user who creates meaning through use. Meaning is what gives housing specificity as part of the manner in which it is used. And so we need to shift the location and focus of our thoughts indoors and stop the pretence that the façade is all there is.

Mere shelter – the brick box that covers us – does not encourage us to stay. We need more than the physicality of shelter to make us feel at home. Thinking properly on housing forces us to look inwards. It makes us look at what goes on within the walls of brick, such that the physicality of shelter is not apparent to us.

To think on housing will take us to the care that comes from use and the acceptance that allows for complacency, such that we lose sight of the physical presence of housing.

We object to the very idea that we are rooted. But while we do this objecting we are determined to stay exactly in place. We need the sanctity of the care-full place in order for us to dream of rootlessness. Likewise, we move around in ruts while convincing ourselves we are free to go anywhere we please. And from this – the reality and the dream combined – we can be content.

We become rootless precisely when housing seemingly ceases to care. This is where housing, which we depend on, lacks animation. Animation comes through use, through positive residing-in. Housing excels through use by becoming animated. It moves through engagement and adopts our purpose as its own, such that through use housing is the unthought-of object. Housing gains its wisdom through re-iterative use, as the constancy of effortless care.

Housing tenders itself to meaningfulness through use. Housing becomes the habitual form of complacency. Use flows through housing and fills it. It does so without ambition or purpose. It is a flow: a pure means with no end. Use creates the conditions for its own continuance. It is maintained by its own persistence. Animation is self-fulfilling.

Use is the continued application of an object for our benefit. But use is also directed towards objects. We take, hold and deploy an object, and the re-iteration of this ensures meaningfulness. Need is the habitual consumption of things. Habit creates meaning through familiarity. Use is repetition and continuing on.

The essence of use is continuation. Use is the deployment of what is close for no other reason than its continuation. There need be no purpose, merely a natural association to that which we wish to keep close. Meaningful use needs no pre-thinking. We do things out of habit and they become meaningful because of reiteration. Use negates the passage of time to be replaced by simply keeping on.

Use must be both common and ordinary. But it is also always particular. It is never use in general, even when we all do the same. Housing is regularity within and sameness without. It is free of intention and lacking motive. Uniqueness in housing is a product of use and is not an intrinsic quality. Housing in general exhibits a necessary sameness that identifies it as housing. But anything else is innovation and a by-product of luxury and aspiration. Innovation in housing is a conceit borne out of the belief that we know what housing must be rather than what it really is and does. To innovate is to pre-empt use from the outset. Innovation is an attempt to mould housing by circumscribing use to an external purpose.

Housing lacks sameness only in its specificity to use and user. In every other case it lacks distinction. However, the sameness of housing is a function of our ability to use it as a thing of like essence. But this leads to possibility, not conformity. The meaning of housing comes from its specificity of use, as a singular meaningful object unrelated to the world in general. Otherwise, it would appear as non-sense to us. Housing can be meaningful only in the singular case.

The specific use is always meaningful, never superficial. Use is determined by separation, by exclusion, even as this is common to all. Housing is kindness, a benign shadow that masks us from others. Housing is only superficial to those on the outside, through hiding the specificity of our use to those excluded, such that our complacency is apart from what is beyond housing.

There is no need to distinguish between housing and its use. Housing is an object for use and of use. It is not independent of use. It is the use of the thing that makes it into housing. The term 'empty housing' is thus a reference point for its current use only. This housing still retains the potentiality of use and this latent quality is what maintains it as housing rather than any other thing. It is use that fills housing and animates it. In this way, housing can be haunted by use in its past. Use leaves a trace that we can follow in memory and in the singular artefacts of use.

Use depends on simple occupation, such that *here*, as the specific place, becomes the house where *I* live. We can say then that housing is always *in practice*. Meaningful use can never be hypothetical. It is always characterised by its thereness.

Housing is an object of care. Housing engages with our care, as we ensoul housing through our presence. Care is the animation of housing through collecting together. It is the *being there for* and the *being theirs towards* that can only exist with enclosure. Care is holding close and holding without motive, whereby we hold for no other reason than the closeness that this brings.

Care is benign attention brought forward through use. It is action directed at things we wish to keep close. Care is the protection of what is mine, so that we can use it is as ours and it grows.

Care is our sacrifice to extend ourselves, to make ourselves a greater whole. It is how we live with and for those who deserve our close attention. The nature of housing is to allow for care by sheltering our sacrifice.

Housing itself cannot care, but it leads to care, and care does not exist without the boundary that housing provides. But our housing is always made for us. Housing contains the sense of caring complacently, as if the caring is of no consequence. This is because housing exists for care. Care is the banality that becomes the exceptional. Care creates what is *ours* as habit without precedent.

Housing is quite like love: it is made to be shared, but only with due discrimination. Sharing makes housing grow. So we should see housing as the condition of non-competition. Housing is a non-divisible space of sharing and care. It concentrates care to a single point and allows us to focus it.

Housing contains intimacy and allows for intimacy. Housing provides rigidity to privacy that means intimacy can grow. Intimacy is care gained through sacrifice, through the giving of oneself. We diminish ourselves to make *ours* the greater whole.

What if there is no care? Is this still housing? In a literal sense the answer must be 'yes'. There is still the object. But, we might ask, is there still meaning? Without care, housing ceases to act and do things with and for us. Housing is *care as action*, the activity of enabling and sustaining complacency.

Complacency is the continuing completion of care. Complacency is the maintaining of care. It is the serenity of keeping on, the banality of *just is*. Care is the inchoate sense that we are accepted such that we can accept where we are.

Complacency is *being-for* without struggle. It is the unthought-of care that derives from re-iteration. Complacency is the ordinary enclosure of care as *being theirs*. We are there exclusively for those we wish to include in our enclosure.

Housing is the pattern of care expressed as complacency and exclusion. Housing is regularity, such that complacency is care without statement and without show. Care is not demonstrative, and this is because it is working too hard.

Care is wrapping and enrapture. Housing works through proximity, through close attention. Care is that close attention. It is enclosure that hides what is ours from others without betraying our sameness.

Care needs exclusion before it can enclose us into complacency. Exclusion enables care by reducing it through enclosure. It concentrates care and focuses it. Likewise, exclusion can mend care by focusing us inwards. Exclusion hides care from the transparency of exposure to the external. Housing enables familiarity through proximity and exclusion. Housing, through its implacability, helps us discriminate, and so to show care. Housing elevates care to the banality of the ordinary, and turns care into meaning.

Housing uses a different sense of time. This is due to the enclosure of care. Care stills time as ordinary complacency. Nothing moves and nothing develops. Housing just *is*. The *is-ness* of housing is out of time. It has no use for movement. The essence of housing is as non-event, as routine where use has no foreground but is lost in the generality of the complacent. Housing does not happen as such. It is rather a pattern of stasis, the continuing occurrence of stillness. In the quietness of our self-confinement we wallow in the complacency of our settlement.

The recognition of movement in housing is upheaval. Upheaval makes housing transparent and use becomes a matter of conscious effort, such that complacency is annulled. Care provides a barrier to upheaval by holding us back in place. Care protects housing from the depredations of motive and aspiration.

Use gives meaning to housing through complacency. Complacency is unthinking care, the easiness of responsibility through habit. Use, through time, becomes the reiteration of complacency, such that meaning need neither be questioned nor sought.

To use housing complacently as *ours* is to accommodate those we include as ours. Accommodation is benign acceptance within housing. We coalesce and remain as complacent. Accommodation is care expressed through mutuality as housing expands to accept us. Through accommodation we use housing together as a whole. Accommodation allows for housing to be care-full as meaningful complacency.

Complacency excludes others by indifference through the opacity of boundaries. But complacency is not neglect. It is the inward displacement of interests towards intimacy. Housing is never just for *anybody*. It is always personal, always specific, always *ours*.

Complacency saves housing from quantification by ensuring its specificity and then veiling it in indifference. Complacency means we have no need to wonder or to compare. Housing allows for care as the banality of small intimacies and for the exercise of meaningful trivia. The success of housing therefore goes unreported. It has to remain opaque. Accordingly, the success of housing is always *mine*. It cannot be shared or reattributed. Complacency means outsiders have no voice and can make no contribution without the acquiescence of the complacent. Housing legitimises a general separation – an apartness – by the peculiar particularity of sharing.

Housing is the confinement of complacency. The boundary of housing turns the banality of complacency to meaningfulness. The boundary of housing determines propriety and gives triviality a purpose.

Housing in its complacency unravels sentiment from anxiety. Complacency allows us to condescend towards aspiration. It prevents housing from becoming competition. Complacency is never comparative. It has no gradation: complacency either exists or it does not.

Housing is always ordinary. It can never be exceptional. To suggest it is exceptional is to be guilty of trespass and to see complacency as directed action.

Complacency is weightless and can have no malice. It does not contrive. It never thinks. It remains in place, unthinking and unthought of. It is quietly accepting of what accepts it.

Housing does not actively engage us. It settles us, calms us, hides us and teaches us not to worry about what is outside. Housing works best when we do not notice our need of it. Housing is fulfilment and so the creation of complacency.

The value of housing cannot be counted. Much of its value is yet to come, through care of what is yet to exist. Yet there is no 'futures market' in complacency and acceptance. Complacency is the acceptance of a real continuous present as an unthought-of space.

Much of what we remember is sifted from the wreckage of loss but filtered by the comfort of our current complacency into pieces small enough for us to manage. We use housing to contain our regrets and make them manageable. Housing moderates, straightens, signifies, adds distance and makes us safe. Housing is always in its place. It can always accept where it is.

Housing cannot be perfect and need not be. It simply has to be enough. Housing has the capacity for both accommodation and acceptance and this allows it to manage diversity.

Housing is the acceptance of care as complacent attention. Acceptance is where implacability encloses us. We have ceased to fight what is around us and so it can now safely and benignly contain us as an accepting being. Housing has no need for decision or indecision, just complacency. We just reside within acceptance. Acceptance is where we give without having to notice what we might take.

Acceptance stills us and leaves us in place. Acceptance reveals housing to be the mutuality of taking. We sincerely offer and we sincerely take, and so we fit in place. Acceptance is only ever mutual. It means we are never totally alone, and because of this we can be still. Acceptance denies the possibility of aspiration. Aspiration is made redundant because of acceptance.

Acceptance is where implacability can be benign. Acceptance is enframing. Housing enframes but casts no shadow. There is no hostility in the well-worn frame. It is grooved by use and warm to the touch. The frame is the comforter because acceptance makes for calm. Housing comes with its edges rounded. It can always find room for sentiment and the benevolent gesture.

Acceptance is to show an open honest face. Acceptance is not acquiescence. It is mutual, a sharing of respect that keeps us in place. We never truly have what we cannot accept. And unless we accept, it can never fully accept us. Housing makes no sense, and remains non-sense, until you accept it as it is.

Acceptance teaches us that each house is greater than the sum of housing. *My* house is the only one. Housing gives us something to be constant about. Housing confines space to make it bearable for us. Housing is not attainment but continuation. It allows us to go on, even as we believe we have stopped. We are driven by safety and comfort, and on to stasis.

We live in the banality of the ordinary. We act and use things in the way we do simply because we can. Life, for most of us, most of the time, is not a struggle. We are not involved in a constant battle with others for resources, or for supremacy over the earth. Our lives are not a fight for the survival of the fittest, or a war of all against all. Most of us, most of the time, find we can just get on and do much of what we want. We can do this without being inconvenienced and without inconveniencing others, and we would be surprised if life were really any other way. Life is not always, or even often, difficult. Things just are, and we can accept that this is simply the way the world is.

When we look at the world we see it as we always have done. We do not expect it to be radically changed from the last time we ventured out, nor do we have to recreate it every time we look. The world is simply the way it is and we know this to be the case. We know of things today because of what we did and saw yesterday and the day before that. We are so certain of this that we do not even have to recognise the fact that things do not change. We need not describe a world that continues to be present for us.

The use we make of things does not have to be obviously meaning-ful. We do not tend to reflect on the present and say, '*What I am doing now is significant, important and meaningful*'. Rather, what matters is the doing itself. The typicality, regularity and the very complacency of the action means that it can be fulfilling without its significance becoming apparent to us. It is something we find ourselves doing with-out necessarily knowing why or being able to see its significance. We need not reflect on the significance of every action, and indeed to do so would put a stop to many of our activities. Our actions are fulfilling in themselves; we have no need to assign them any further intention or purpose. They are worth doing for their own sake without any other justification. What is meaningful is that we can do these things without having to think about them or see them as significant in themselves.

Many of the things we do are ends in themselves. We have no ulterior motives and our actions are not the means to an end. Our friendships are not intended to secure anything other than the camaraderie of the moment and our hobbies are pursued for their immediate enjoyment. There is no particular purpose to the action: we are just living and using what is around us to help us do so. This is how housing works.

We do not always notice what we are using. We do not tend to see an object as differentiated from us as we use it. The object becomes an extension of us while we use it. It works with us and does so without appearing to be separate or distinct. While it works with us, it is just there, it operates as a part of us and it cannot be distinguished from us. Clearly such an object has significance, but this significance is not apparent. It is only when the object breaks or we lose the capacity to use it that we become aware of it.

In order to live as we do, we must be complacent. We do not often test ourselves and we do not reflect on what we do. We feel secure and safe in what we are and where we are. As such, we are able to absorb experiences and to accommodate them as part of our ordinary world.

The notion of complacency might be taken as a negative. It can mean extreme self-satisfaction and smugness. It is where we are pleased with ourselves, self-righteous and unconcerned with anything other than ourselves. These might not be seen as virtues and so we can wonder why we might see them as important, and even necessary, to us. But smugness and a lack of concern are traits noticed by others, and we may not see ourselves as they do. Due to housing's implacability we do not notice the views of others and how we are perceived. Instead we are more concerned with our own priorities and with care for those we are close to. And in doing this, we get a sense of a life well led. Our sense of complacency, then, is where we are calmly content. We can become absorbed in our own world and feel no need to be questioned over our legitimate actions.

Our sense of complacency allows us to absorb elements from outside and to incorporate them into our ordinary lives without necessarily feeling that we are changing. When we absorb something, this implies that we soak it up or assimilate it. It might mean that we consume the thing from outside, but also we might be extended by it. We have taken in the force of the external object and have grown or changed as a result. But because we have incorporated it, we see it as already part of us rather than as a distinct addition. So the importance of the idea of absorption is that it carries no sense of an expansion or extension of our sense of the ordinary. We are like a sponge in the way we can soak up material without appearing to expand ourselves beyond our natural limits. We are able to retain a sense of balance. We are not pushed to extremes of taste or action but can keep a certain ambivalence, a detachment from commitment, and hold each element together in a composed whole.

What appears to be negative from the outside, from the standpoint of a person looking at us who does not understand us and seeks to view us according to some objective criteria, might be entirely positive from an internal, subjective point of view. Indeed, ambivalence is a necessary part of complacency, in that it is the external appearance of our complacent self. When we are operating as our ordinary selves, we will appear to be absorbed in our interests and ends, and this means holding together a number of elements that form the habitual frame of our lives. From the outside this will appear as a lack of commitment or as a lack of decisiveness with regard to the world around us. We do not notice things in their objectivity, as elements distinct from us, but we absorb them into the on-going habits and routines that make up our sense of the ordinary.

Housing always waits for us. It will not leave us behind, and it can warm us even when we are absent. That little corner is always still there. Wherever we are, our housing is close by. We still feel its presence around us. It befalls on housing to repair us, even as we neglect it. Housing welcomes the warmth of coming together and it does not want us to be alone: that is why it has doors.

But doors can be locked and windows can be barred and, in their time, they must be. Housing is also a barrier that protects intimacy and allows us to care in unthought-of complacency. Housing externalises anonymity by its implacability. This is how implacability protects and enhances complacency. This is through deflection, whereby housing is anonymised, so it appears only for us. For all but the user, housing is non-specific, non-identifiable and merely one of an uncountable mass. Its uniqueness is only properly manifested to the user through their own use.

When we look out from housing our gaze is always framed. All matters regarding housing ultimately derive from the fact that it is enclosed. Actions take place *inside* and away from the world. All we can know about housing *as housing* flows from this one insight.

Housing stands, and from this our understanding can grow. This is the point of housing: that it stands. The stillness of housing masks us and allows us to move at will. As such, the immobility of housing is as much a mentality as a physical condition. Wherever we are, it accommodates us. We know we can return, in memory if not always in fact.

We should embrace the stillness that housing brings to us. The implacability of housing – the fact that it just stands – is not disregard but opportunity. Exclusion provides us with a front for our intimacy. Housing enlightens through its weight, and because it is opaque. The opacity of the boundaries given by housing allows us a space for non-reflection.

We close the door on contention and live alike. We can accommodate those whom we feel we can ignore. But only because it is mutual. We show we welcome the indifference of our neighbours by offering them our own indifference. We care for them by giving them the space and opportunity to ignore us.

Housing helps us find obscurity in its sameness. Housing hides the eccentricity of our intentions and gives us all the chance to be normal. It can have no cunning, only a precision in its response. Housing takes up no direction. It can face any way.

Housing is just as welcoming to the worst of us. It cannot have judgement and remain implacable. Housing remains constant, even as we let it down with our changes of mind, our uncertainty and our dilettantism. Housing absolves us of responsibility by giving us the illusion that we are taking charge.

Housing asks for nothing and cannot take anything but that which it is given. Housing is never creative. It is only ever orthodox. Housing is never afraid of appearing normal, or of excluding the strange. It knows who pays the bills. Housing, in all its variety, is a testament to predictability.

Our housing is never strange. We can always dismiss the context of our own eccentricities even as we gape at the strangeness of others. Housing has specificity but not originality. We must be able to recognise it as housing. Housing always resembles how it once was. That is why we always tend to remember our childhood.

Housing is always only habitual. But it is also habit forming. Housing forms habits and so becomes habit. We cannot have anything habitual without housing. Housing shapes our habits, which have to bend themselves around it.

Housing can never be free of us, and we can never be free of it. To eschew housing is a form of suicide. Accordingly, implacability is not ambivalence. It is too determined and too certain to act for any doubt.

Intimacy fails when housing is transparent. Exclusion allows for the expression of intimacy. Housing, properly speaking, can never be public. This would mean it becomes transparent and so loses its ability to contain and enclose. The outward face of housing should always be implacable. It should reserve its favours to those who can properly cross its threshold. Housing's welcome must be rationed for it to remain as housing.

Exclusion is not based on title but on a boundary. It is not control but benign indifference: the inability, and lack of desire, to look in. Exclusion is the actuality of complacency. Housing is never itself kind, but it makes for kindness. The hardness of housing can be sheltering.

Closeness, living near-by and living the same, can be the perfect barrier. It forces us to look the other way. It ensures that we ignore others as we focus on ourselves.

There is no ending to housing. It cannot match our own finitude. Housing keeps its own time: slow, cyclical, rhythmic. Housing demands regularity that delimits the flow of time. Time cannot escape from housing.

Housing is always close and distant; inclusive and exclusive; welcoming and implacable, and always consistent. Implacability is not aggression or obstruction, but the hardness of passivity.

Housing appears soft until it is tested. Housing lets us mark it, push it and pull it. It will not fight us. But its patience is not infinite. It too has its limits. Any apparent shallowness of housing is due to our ability to move. We mistake movement for depth.

Implacability is housing just standing. It can include or exclude; it can be open or closed. It can stand firm with us inside or outside. Implacability is a relation based on the physicality of housing and of our need to reside within it. But implacability does not argue, it merely stands.

Implacability is the still and unyielding face. It is a mix of the passive and the rigid. The opacity of the unfeeling object can be good or bad.

Implacability masks the limit of understanding, of not knowing at which point things will give way. Acceptance is where we choose not to test these limits. Housing teaches us not go to extremes. We have no need to stretch beyond the ordinary. We have nothing to gain by breaking out of housing's limits.

The implacability of housing supports the dominant condition. It does not make choices for us. It can only magnify our chosen effects through passive reflection. Implacability is neither kindness nor unkindness. It is passive stasis that helps or hinders, depending on from where we push it.

Housing gives us the leisure and comfort to ignore all those really important things others apparently have to dwell on. Housing helps us to hide without ever feeling we are lost. Housing allows us to hide even from ourselves. Housing is a respite from our impotence. For a time, housing makes us all-powerful. It leaves us unopposed and exonerates us from the need for justification. It is the very ordinariness of housing that makes it special, and it means that we can all use it and use it all the time, and not really notice what we are doing, and there is no reason why we have to explain our actions to anyone else, even if we could.

Housing exists because sometimes there is just too much world. In housing we can lose ourselves without having to go anywhere. It lets us share our aloneness with those we love.

Without housing would we ever be truly alone? Housing gives us the means to be properly alone. We can even share our aloneness with others. Housing means others can always find us, but it also means that we do not have to look at them. We can trust to the indifference of others every time we lock our door, while our indifference frees them.

We can celebrate that our house is special to no one other than ourselves. We can thank others for their indifference. Housing is the most effective way we have to make ourselves harmless to others. Our boundaries limit what we can do to others, just as the boundaries prevent others from impinging on us. But this opacity can allow us to harm others and ourselves within its boundaries. Again we can see the implacability that is housing.

Exclusion is necessary to make us whole. Housing spares us the trouble of having to remake ourselves daily. Without it we cannot share with impunity. We are protected by our own anonymity.

The reliability of housing allows us to remain unnoticed while believing we are still being useful and of some significance. We can be grateful that housing lacks intensity. Housing makes struggle optional. It reduces a cause to a choice and we are able to take advantage of its neutrality.

Choice only matters when it is granted. That is why we have boundaries. Choice, unlike duty, is always extrinsic. It depends on where we are and what surrounds us. And it is the boundaries of housing that make obligation easier to bear.

Housing does not need to shun. It can rely on the indifference of others. Housing need be no more than polite. It has no need for dialogue and refuses debate. It does not contest or contend. It will politely ignore us, and will expect us to do the same.

We hide from the world, in our little corner, because the world demands that we do. Complacency on the inside is a result of indifference on the outside. Indifference presents no different face, merely the dull unappealing face of implacability. It is neither yours nor mine – until it is either. Housing is care because it allows us to be ignored by others, just as we ignore them.

Inclusion gives a purpose to exclusion, such that we do not notice what others are doing around us. Housing helps us hide our meanings from all objections. It reduces complaint to rubble. Housing cushions the consequences of our own beliefs by forcing politeness on others. It is our place and sharing has its limits.

But housing is background, and that it what it is meant to be. It should not be the focus of our attention. It is the stage and not the action. But it is what makes the illusion work.

Housing just stands. It stands in rows, compliant, waiting and unmoved. Housing offers us an oasis from progress and the need to change. It makes no demands on us and welcomes us despite our intentions. Housing means we can stop. Housing is a long-held possession that keeps us for as long as we need it to.

Housing is never an abyss. It is always containing. We lose it; it does not lose us. We can walk away; it cannot. Housing can only respond. Its condition depends on where we start and where we go.

Housing's concreteness is essential, but it is still incidental to its meaning. It is essential because of its opacity, which therefore allows use. The concreteness of housing is instrumental.

Housing is fixed. It is static and remains in place. We are in place. This may not always be in the same place. We may move, but this moving is not housing. It is merely moving to another place. Housing becomes housing when it is fixed.

But then do not all of us need to be housed? Why are there apparent exceptions to the need to be fixed? We do not ignore these exceptions by stating them as such. Rather we show their significance, and in doing so we are able to maintain the significance of both the norm and the exception. We should not seek to diminish either housing or those exceptions to it. Both are particular and meaningful in their ordinariness to those who have use of them. The exceptions to housing demonstrate housing in its fixity, and the fixity of housing demands we give attention to those not fixed. We have no need to diminish the exceptions as, through their own uniqueness, they show the nature of housing as fixed. But we do harm to the fixity of housing in diminishing it in the aid of the exceptional.

Housing can only remain close to us. It is always particular and local. It does not take us by surprise. It cannot do this and be housing. It is always there, always necessary.

Housing does not go anywhere. That is its greatest strength, and its greatest limit. Housing is regularity, consistency and constancy. There are no surprises. Housing holds what moves. But housing never moves.

For us, but only for us, housing has no periphery: it is all centre. Yet, housing is gloriously aimless. It has no direction, no purpose. It is us, but only for us, that strip away the benign and try to focus.

When we leave our shell does it no longer resound? We find it hard to imagine housing without us. Does this make us selfish?

The implacability of housing is essentially passive. It cannot fight back. It can only resist but soon it will crack and break. But we cannot benefit from this. We are now nothing more than the average invader, showing our anger at an object no longer capable of helping us.

Chapter 4
Misuse

Housing just stands and so it is a hostage to our intentions. Housing is an objectless object. The only ambition it contains is our own. It can therefore be prey to our aspirations and desires. To aspire is to compete with housing instead of working with it. It is to abuse it instead of using it. Aspiration breaks housing by trying to force it to move. The activity of aspiration is policy.

Aspiration is the sponsoring of a motive that takes us outside. It teaches us to be wary of where we are for fear of where we wish to be. Aspiration is dissatisfaction with here and now. Aspiration leaves housing cold. Housing is implacable to the speed of impressions.

Aspiration makes us too aware of housing. But what do we see? What is it, or what do we think it could be? Aspiration is where we deign to be as implacable as the housing we reside in. But housing does not know how to acquiesce and so the result is conflict in which housing is damaged. When housing becomes damaged we will always lose. Gaps will appear, perhaps just a crack, but this is still too much for our illusions. If housing means nothing, it becomes nothing.

Aspiration causes a hollowing out of housing. Aspiration carves housing into a new and unnatural shape, turning its welcome into an unfriendly competitive glare. Aspiration is where we expect to take more than we wish to give. It is selfishness. Aspiration is to hold housing hostage and to ransom it for an illusive future. It is the desire to be elsewhere, to use housing as collateral.

Cost and value are the products of aspiration. Measurement makes housing a cold place, reducing cradling to counting. We spend so much time discussing cost and value we lose sight of why we might want housing in the first place. We forget that cost and value are incidental to use, and that we can use housing despite these. Administering to wealth leaves housing unfinished, making its meaning common and apparent to all. This apparentness calls housing into question. It attaches motive to housing and housing becomes derivative. Motive externalises the practice of housing, monetising it while casting its gaze onto another.

Aspiration creates wariness towards housing and in housing. We are now using housing for the purpose of another thing. We no longer care for *this one thing* – for the only house we can have now. We become wary of it because we are not using it for itself. It has become an object of cost and value. As a result the meanings we attach to housing are elsewhere.

Aspiration is the attempt to get beyond housing and to believe that there can be something more. It reduces housing to something that is merely materially instrumental, and implies that it has no meaning that cannot be counted.

Motive becomes the enemy of complacency by questioning the meaningful use of housing as complacent care. It brings the object-hood of housing to the fore and makes it consequential. Housing, as such, becomes an unavoidable burden. Motive shifts care onto hous-ing as an object and prevents acceptance. Housing itself then replaces meaningful use and becomes quantified as an object. Housing in its true nature is then lost. It stops being a means for the enclosure of care, and instead housing now appears to be derived from the external.

Motive circumscribes the current use of housing by the demands of tomorrow. Motive is to see purpose in what is just here now before us. It forces us to look outside. Housing becomes conditional and based on wariness rather than care. Wariness means we prevaricate over use such that it becomes transparent and calculable. Use is reduced to finiteness by motive. Once housing becomes conditional it demands a purpose that takes it beyond housing. Housing becomes a pure object and its implacability becomes a form of resistance that threatens the integrity of use and deflates meaning.

Wariness is the manipulation of use through calculation, such that acceptance is withdrawn and housing becomes transparent as motive. Wariness is where the meaning is externalised as purpose. Housing is reduced to a quantity to be weighed by external purpose. Meaning is shifted to the material; it is solidified as purposeful intent.

Motive wears housing as a symbol of status. Motive turns housing into a performance. It reduces it to show by externalising it and open-ing it out as spectacle.

Aspiration affects those who depend on us. It is where egoism domi-nates. Egoism involves not the denigration of the self, but the denigra-tion of others. It is where we take our own significance to denote our superiority over others. We are too important to be concerned about others. This is not because of a misguided view of the unimportance of others, but is rather due to an inability to see that our own significance indicates the equal significance of all others. We are therefore prepared to use others as the means to fulfil our own ends in the misguided belief that our ends are superior. Others are subsidiary to us, and they can be reduced to material that we feel able to mould as we wish.

The use of others often does not take the form of cold calculation or involve overt cruelty. It may not take the form of slavery, but may be simply a case of a lack of sight. We just do not see the needs of others, nor do we appreciate the effect that our actions have on others. We are so engrossed with our own significance that we are blind to the effects of our actions have on others.

This form of materialisation depends on our ability to dominate others. There is always the potential for conflict between rival egoisms. This means that materialisation will most often take place in private spaces rather than in public. Public conflict can be policed and rival egoisms regulated. But in the private sphere there will only tend to be self-regulation and self-control. Moreover, it is precisely within the private sphere where imbalances between rival egoisms will be at their greatest, particularly between parent and child. One adult may not be able to use another as a commodity in the public sphere, yet a parent may use a child as such within the domestic environment. Children can become possessions that are consumed, such that we do not live for our children, but they live for us. We do not bend to their expectations, but they are shaped by ours. Children become things that we own, symbols of our egoism and means by which we manifest our own selves. We do not do this deliberately or in any cruel and calculating manner. Rather, we insist simply that our egoism be expressed and that nothing be allowed to hamper it. Housing allows us to dominate others and to promote our egoism through motive, such that children can fall prey to the aspirations of adults.

We can picture care-full housing by its imperturbability, by its stability, stasis and complacency. Yet when the transience of aspiration enters, what leaves is stability. The still waters are troubled, and become perturbed. Housing struggles to cope with aspiration because it is built to deal with the external threat, to protect what is inside from what is outside. Yet now the threat comes from within.

This pressure built up from within cannot be naturally released: the enclosure that is housing prevents it. The strength of enclosure can absorb much, and the stores of care can withhold a great deal, yet the walls are built to keep things out and to hold us safe within. What may happen then is a leakage, a failure of the insulation, an unnatural break in the fabric of housing. But this too breaks all the intimacy, the security, the stability, and things start to move, perhaps all too quickly, out of our control, and we are found to be foolish for our complacency. Housing is easier to destroy from within, using those elements subversive of complacency. Housing can be undermined through the selfishness of the internal gaze that places the egoism of aspiration above care.

If we will not care for housing, why should it care for us? Housing is without motive, without an end. Its purpose is in continuation. It need promise nothing; it has already delivered. We should comfort ourselves, then, by holding onto the thought that tomorrow's housing has already been built.

The result of aspiration is policy. Once there is an external purpose there is a need to act. Policy exists for the satiability of aspiration. But policy is always outside of housing. A concern for housing policy is like having an interest in food and looking at how it is grown, harvested, processed, distributed and priced, but then having absolutely no interest in what it tastes like. Housing policy is only concerned with the creation and distribution of housing. It neglects to consider that actually we wish to use housing, and that this is what principally matters to us.

We should not allow housing to be diminished or made subservient to any other element, be it policy or design. Housing must be provided and the means found to pay for it. Housing must be designed and built. But just as agriculture is not food, so policy and design are not housing, and neither can they tell us what housing does. We can only understand what housing does by how the objects are used and how they relate to those who use them. Elements outside of housing cannot help us here. Indeed we need to recognise that the reverse is actually the case: an understanding of what housing is and what it does is necessary to properly undertake policy and design. The proper relations need to be observed such that we see both policy and design as subsidiary and dependent on housing.

Policy cannot see housing as *mine*. It always sees housing as neutralised, depersonalised and emptied out. Policy can only see housing as potential, never as fulfilment. It takes housing to be uniform and use to be irrelevant. Once housing is built, policy forgets about it. But use begins with the *there-ness* of housing and so shows what housing does, while policy, for the user, withers away to irrelevance.

Policy mistakes the material for meaning and so diminishes housing to a single point in time. Policy ignores the continuity of housing. Housing has a constancy that supplants the immediacy of policy. That housing stands in its own time brings into question the imperative of policy.

Housing and policy exist in different frames of time. The slowness of housing refuses to be affected by the frenetic nature of policy. Housing allows for an avoidance of planning while ensuring the future for us. Housing is a perpetual *here*. Housing has a longevity that allows us to focus continually on the present.

Policy leads to rigidity by being purposive. It assumes that use is predetermined and can be patterned externally. Policy can only ever create a simple purpose. It does not recognise that housing can grow as it will through use.

We should not confuse housing with 'community' any more than we should confuse it with 'policy' or 'design'. A focus on community, as with policy, is to reduce housing to a subsidiary. Housing exists despite, not because of, community. Community is not particular enough to allow for housing as such. Community is not the same as housing. We should not talk of 'housing communities', but only of housing, and refuse to define housing in terms not directly associated to its actual use. We might acknowledge that community can affect use and meaning, but only *after* there is housing and not as a cause. Community does not determine housing or make it necessary.

Policy attempts to remake housing as 'homes': as an aggregate based on standards. The reduction of housing to aggregates and standards makes it a transparent void. It can no longer hold anything meaningful. Aggregation trivialises housing through standardisation, while dis-aggregation demonstrates the significance of housing through its very unique ordinariness. We might say that the word 'home' has become a sentimentalised adjunct to policy. Home no longer has the meaning that we should associate with it. It has been reduced to an aggregation of the material, to the idea of 'homes'. To make home into a plural is to empty it out of all meaning. We should refuse to use it in this manner and return to home as a reference to meaningful use, or stop using the word at all.

Aggregation turns housing into a calculation capable of completion. It carries within it the assumption that housing can be finished. Housing becomes a problem that can be solved, a crisis that can be ameliorated. Aggregation implies that housing can be dealt with as if it were an equation.

Aggregation makes housing comparative and therefore competitive. It sees housing as a resource, as a quantity. Aggregation turns housing into a competition, a battle for resources and the determination to maximise assets. Housing loses its shape, its distinctive form, when it becomes aggregated. It can then only be differentiated numerically.

To preserve housing as an asset is to become wary of it, to attach motive to what is best left unthought of. We move from care to a concern for value, to where housing is reduced to a mere asset. Seeing housing as an asset is to assume it is disposable, and to make its disposability its purpose.

As an asset housing becomes negotiable. It becomes contingent and relative to some other thing. Housing ceases to matter *as housing*, and we stop using it for care and think about value; to value housing as an aggregate is to diminish it. The quantification of housing empties it of meaning. It externalises and monetises it. We no longer use housing for care, but 'care' for housing in general. Housing, properly speaking, cannot be a commodity and remain meaningful. It no longer encases care, but becomes an object divorced from the particularity of use.

To see housing as an asset is to assume that it can be moved, that it is tradable. It has to become known, it has to be transparent. Housing is forced to perform, to demonstrate itself. It can no longer rely on mutual indifference and so we become wary of its use.

The sameness of housing is a benign irrelevance until it is monetised. Sameness is not aggregation. Sameness is doing common things apart. Aggregation is non-differentiation, the indifferent collation of housing into an imagined whole. Sameness, until it is monetised, is what allows us to act as we will, while aggregation, by standardising housing to homes, demands that we act in a specific manner. Aggregation de-animates housing. It can only see housing as an empty shell. It sees sameness as quantitative and not qualitative.

Policy is contestation; housing is resolution. Policy is finitude; housing is constancy. Policy is direction; housing is stasis. Policy is sentimental; housing is implacable. Housing is more than a monetised shell. Housing is beyond value, beyond calculation.

Chapter 5
The consequences of use

The way that we come to the world is not always direct. Often we come to the world through memory. We are walking along a beach talking and laughing, and as we discuss what interests us we catch sight of a shell in the sand near our feet. The colour of this shell, a sort of metallic sheen of purples and pinks like a bruise in metal, transfixes us and so we stop to pick it up and we turn it over in our hands, rubbing the sand off. We find the shell pleasing to touch because of its warmth and smoothness. As we turn it in our hand it catches the sun and glints, and it still appeals when we have the measure of it, its shape, weight and feel, and so we keep it and put it in our pocket as we carry on walking. Weeks later, when we are back at home, we catch sight of it again where we left it on the bookshelf, and as we look at it we remember where we found it and who we were with, and why being in that place at that time mattered to us so much. The shell has become a store of memory and so we do not just remind ourselves of how it feels to the touch, but also now we think of the occasion when we found it, of who we were talking to, what we might have said, the particulars of place and weather, and the feel of the day as we experienced it. All of this can come from this found object that just happened to be there at that time but now has a purpose. This is as a trigger of memory that opens up our thoughts and feelings and allows us remember the time, the person and the place.

§

The notions of *where* and *when* are always together. Time and space cannot be separated; one depends on the other. This is what Mikhail Bakhtin meant by his idea of the chronotope, the idea of time and place linked in memory. He defines this concept (which literally means 'time-space') as 'the intrinsic connectedness of temporal and spatial relationships that are artistically expressed in literature'.[1] The artist aims to connect time and space into one, and where it works well, 'Time, as it were, thickens, takes on flesh, becomes artistically visible; likewise, space becomes charged and responsive to the movements of time, plot and history'.[2] What this meant for Bakhtin was that questions of the self could be dealt with only when seen as questions of specific location. Our sense of self, or our history, is also our sense of time and place, and this is always specific. We have no experiences outside of time and place. This is to suggest that time is stopped and put into a particular place. Memories, in other words, are always located.

As we move through life we move from place to place. We meet new people and drift away from others. Partnerships form and break up and parents die, leaving their children to make their own way. Over time we find that there are places from which we are now cut off and people whom we can no longer contact. This means that a lot of the knowledge that is important to us, such as the things we did as children, in places we can now only half remember, is now lost. That knowledge rests with people who are now deceased and they have taken their knowledge with them, and we may now have no means of finding those other people and places who once were important to us. Our parents die and take their memories and their knowledge of us as children with them. This loss is no doubt minor when compared to physical loss of loved ones, but over time we come to realise that not only are these people now gone but so are the places that we shared, and particularly the places that formed us. We have lost the people who raised us, but also the places in which we were together. All we now have left are our own memories of people and places, which we can no longer corroborate.

We can still remember these places. But they are lost. Perhaps not in the literal sense of no longer existing, but they might as well be. We now have no grounds to be there, and no means of locating them now that our main guides have gone. Our parents, who made these places and who led us through them, are no longer capable of guiding us. The people who created the distinctiveness of these places are no longer next to us, and so even if we could return to physical locations they would be empty.

Yet the older we get the more important it is to try to excavate our memories and find our way back to these places, partly because this helps to maintain any link with the people we have lost. But it is also

1 Bakhtin (1981), p. 84.
2 Bakhtin (1981), p. 84.

because these places become more tantalising as the distance grows, and as we realise that it has been these places that have made us what we are. Emile Cioran in his early book *Tears and Saints* makes the following claim:

> The more you advance in life, the more you realise that you don't learn anything, you just go back in memory. It is as if we reinvent a world in which we once lived. We don't gain anything, we just regain ourselves. Self-identity is reverse evolution.[3]

As we grow older we go backwards and regain ourselves through memory. We piece ourselves together through attempts at recollection, as if we are picking up a trail of fragments as we seek to return home. We seek to return to the source of our memories, to those places where we were together with those now gone. It is through remembering that we try to recreate ourselves, or, perhaps better said, to reinvent our history as meaningful relationships with those we have known and loved.

So this is an exercise in excavation, of digging back into the past to find places that have been lost. Through memory we seek to get back into places and renew them. And in these places are people, and these people are what make these places matter.

§

But when these places and people do come back they are not as they were. This is because the very act of recreation alters them, through the selectivity of the process, through wishful thinking, and through the large element of *me as I am now* that goes into this purportedly old place. We (re)create these old places as if they were new through the association with new relations and the state in which we now find ourselves. What we know now, how we feel now, and whom we are now with, all condition this creation of places.

The work of memory is not merely introspection, but retrospection. It is about thinking about how things were in the past tense and bringing them into the present. It concerns the representation of places back to ourselves. It is about how places now can appear and what they become when we combine the present and the past.

What we recollect, and what we can find from conversations with others still here, from photographs and from dredging back in memory, is always partial. All we can ever get are small bits and pieces of a

3 Cioran (1995), p. 17.

life. And we see these distant places through a lens, and like all lenses it restricts the view to a narrower angle, and within a defined frame. The lens needs to be focussed and indeed to be pointing right where it should. We have to know what to look for and where we might find it. So we might not focus properly, or even look at the right thing, never mind that we might not fit it all in the frame. We might zoom in because we wish to see it better, but in doing so we might lose some perspective, or cut out something else that is significant. When we look back it is always partial.

What tempers our looking back is our intentions, and these, in turn, are determined by where we are now. Only by being in the right place can we obtain a good view, and this is hardly ever guaranteed. So what matters is what we are looking at, what we are looking at it through, and where we are looking at it from. Where we are may not be the best place to stand. But of course, this is where we are stuck, and this is the case even if the view is obscured, or the object is too distant, and we have to peer above, around or through other objects to see it. Whole forests, more recently planted, may now be in the way.

We cannot, then, remember a place as it actually was then, nor can we remember it as *we* were then, and this is because we are not there now and not the same person as then. Our memories are cluttered by our own histories, and we cannot circumvent this, and we cannot replace it or reject it. We cannot simply unknow the history that sits between us now and us then. So it is not just that our memories are partial, but that they are cluttered up with other material. The memories we want to find might be hidden behind other things, and might now have been given different associations by what has come after.

Yet despite this we can regain parts of memory, we can recall bits of our past more fully and clearly. We can often do this because there is an imperative – a yearning – to remember that drives us forward trying to uncover as much as we can. Indeed, what perhaps drives us most to remember is precisely the fact that the object of our memory is now partially hidden, so that we cannot remember it as we would like to. We know these things to be significant, we really feel it, but we just cannot see it all as we think we ought, and so we drive ourselves on to find more.

Of course, something starts this desperation, and this is often the physical loss of someone who is close, and who has shared this place with us. Not only do we lose the person, but we have also lost the ability to have the trite and apparently inconsequential conversations about our shared past, the ability to simply talk with them or ask them about something, somewhere or someone. We are now permanently estranged from them and this cannot be altered in any way. They are gone and all we have to rely on are our own memories. Part of what we were, and still like to think that we are, is now cut off from us. As well as this close person, we have lost their store of memory and so things that we could gain access to are now, if not totally lost, then in serious danger of being so. We must now rely on our own wits and memory. We have to work harder to maintain connections to the past ourselves. It is now only us who can do the work, for no one is there to help us, to lead us, to call out directions to us. We have to find the place ourselves, and we have lost part of the map.

But it is precisely when they cease to be there that we feel we have to start to look. It is only then, when access to that place is really endangered and cannot just be touched by a casual remark from a loved one, that we are overtaken by a desperation to find ourselves *with* them. If only we were in that place, if we could still be there, then we would not have the aching loss, and have no need to search. We could just reach out and hold on to that person; we could be there with them. What we cannot do now is just take things for granted. We now have to work for our memories instead of just relying on the casual remark and the ready answer. Instead, we are left to yearn for what has gone in the hope that this will remake us as whole.

We know that these places, and these people, are what helped to make us and so we are looking for our place in the past and, in doing so, we believe it will locate us fully in the present. It is only with this full presentness, which includes all that is past, all our history, that we are whole. This includes all that we call the 'past' as well as all that which is past. For us, the past is both *a* place and a store *of* places, a somewhere and a collection of specific *heres*.

§

When we see a photograph of someone we know – say, of our parents when they were young – one of the first things we tend to ask is, 'Where was that taken?' One of the key means we have to understand an image is to locate it, to place the people in that image in the particular setting. This helps us to make sense of it; to find the sense, as it were, in the picture. Do we feel we know the people in the photo better because we now know the place? Perhaps if we have been there too this somehow validates it, strengthens the link we have with the people in it? Seeing them in a familiar place maintains a bond. The knowledge of place offers some link, so that we can absorb more of these people into our experience.

But can we be sure of any memory that has been sparked off by an image? Are we projecting the image into our memory, putting something in there that wasn't there before? Or is it a case of the image bringing forward memories of the place and the people? Perhaps it is simply that the more we dwell on a place or a person, the more of that place or person seems to return to us.

Whether real or planted, the memory is always just a fragment, and in this way memory is like a photograph. A photograph is the result of looking through a viewfinder, which allows us to see what we wish to stop and memorialise, but which also frames and so circumscribes it. A memory is not complete. There is a mist, a shadowy framing, around the image. Is this through the focusing on the important part of the image, or is it a lack in memory, its partiality, so that only bits have been kept? We have cropped the photos; or better, we have torn the extraneous edges away to leave only the centre so we can focus on the one thing that seems to matter.

The frame presents us with a border of significance: that within the frame is what matters and is imbued with meaning, whilst that outside it is now deemed irrelevant. What is beyond the frame is now completely lost to us. A frame may well be contrived and show the artificiality of an image. Indeed the act of framing can be entirely arbitrary and contingent, but it still acts to sort out the images and therefore to define things, so that what is 'in frame' or has been 'enframed' becomes significant because it is that which is presented to us, or which we, if we were the image maker, have chosen to present.

But this metaphor of the frame can only take us so far. In memory the frame is rather ill-defined, and perhaps porous, in that we are never sure if one image has not leaked into another, that we have not framed something of a composite of images from different sources. Therefore, the dwelling in our memories does not have the same material palpability, but is more ephemeral and shadowy.

The place we try to remember now has no independence. It has no distinct nature beyond us having been there at one point in time. The real place is now subservient to the memory and this applies even though it was the very particularity of the place and its associations that draw us to it. But now it is as if the place only exists for this memory, that it only matters because of what is now in our head, and it has no other reason to exist. It only now has a meaning for us because of what we experienced there, and we now have no other means of accessing this place other than through this memory. That is how we think we saw it, because that is how we remember it, but we cannot now see it any other way. The place matters because we were there and we did, so we think, see it like that.

The place itself comes to frame the memory even as it is part of it, and so is not really neutral. What we remember took place there, and so the place is part of the memory. But the fact that it took place precisely in that place now compartmentalises and characterises the memory. It can now only take place there, and perhaps we can only see the particular person we are searching for in that place and at that time. The place now seems to keep hold of the memory and so holds that person.

But is this how things actually were? Is the memory really the place we think it is? The enduring sense we have gained of significant people, such as our parents, has been conditioned by the regularity of their continued presence over time, and perhaps over many places. Our parents were not just always there, but they were always doing certain things such that we could depend upon them. But the things we now tend to remember are not general, but are rather very precise. And the memorable times are precisely when our parents did not conform to our complacent vision of them. What we remember is when they apparently acted out of character, or when they behaved in a manner that we would not have expected. What we now dwell on are the exceptions rather the generality of our actual experiences with them. So, we might ask again, are we really remembering them as they were, or are we remembering them as special and distinct from their real selves? What are we leaving out and what are we putting in that place instead?

§

Memories change only in volume, in breadth and depth, but not in how they end. An obvious point, but one we often neglect to consider. We can remember more and better, and the image can appear broader and deeper, but it is still of things that are, in one very important way, fixed. We may remember in colour; the memories can last longer; we can appear to walk through them, like we were in a forest clouded with mist, but always there is the same ending, that same fork in the road, the same decision and so the same conclusion. We can regret that we went left and not right, or that we said one thing and not something better, that we did what we did and that we cannot now negate it or go back on it. We did do all these things we now dwell on. We can speculate on what might have happened, but all these things cannot be changed; there is no way of going back and doing anything again.

But also we know that while any change in the route taken may well have opened up certain things, it would also have closed down others.

We might like to think that we can enjoy the benefits of taking a different decision, but we ignore what would or could not then occur as a result. These dreamed-of openings and foregone possibilities, we need to remember, are always hypothetical, but the closings will always be real and actual. Any change in the route would have meant different relationships and different career choices and prospects. We would have been a different person. This, we might think, would have been better for us and led to a more enjoyable and fulfilling life. But it would have meant foregoing real relationships with people we now know and love. We would not have met those significant people later down the road and, of course, people that we now love, such as our own children, would never have been born. This, for most of us, is an unbearable thought. Thinking about the past, we soon realise, has a hard edge to it and idle speculation can soon turn unpleasant.

So there is a palpable relief when we return to the banal clutter of normal life with the little signs of the veracity of the decisions that we have made. We can relish the reassurance of the consequentiality and responsibility of our decisions as we see these familiar faces in these familiar places. It is these moments, of looking up and seeing what is known and just there, that hold memories back, and which then allow us to place them at a distance. These moments allow us to gain some perspective in the openness of their detail, which shows us that our flights of fancy are only one-dimensional.

Memories have no reverse side. They are blank on the other side, and are, as it were, flat. We might see them at times with an apparent depth, but they are really only flat objects slotted into space and which need us to provide the perspective. Any sense of depth in our memories is an illusion that we substantiate by the manner in which we approach them and how we then look at them. If we were to look at them from a different – objective – direction we would see the flatness, the lack of dimension and the lack of any real relation between the various parts. Memory is based on an illusion, and is always partial, one-sided and incomplete, and so we have to look elsewhere for our depth, for a rounded and full vision of a world that still includes us within it.

Despite our hopes, we are not, if we are really honest, actually *in* memory. Memory is as it were, in us. Memory is a haunting trace. Undoubtedly there can be much joy in this, and we feel pleasure in the recollection of certain things. Yet there is also an ambivalence, a feeling that we are looking at things that are closed and finished, and that there are things that are now completely lost.

But we also know that there are things that were never there, and so there is a partial emptiness made up of all we have not done, those omissions and failures that we now regret. We know that sometimes we could have done more for those who were close to us. There were things we know we should have done, and there are now gaps because we did something else instead. There are things that we would like now to take back and start again.

But we never can go back, and we know that if we were to try we would unravel all that we have ever actually done. We know that all we have done, the omissions, regrets and failures, are all tied together with the successes and happy thoughts, and if we were to try and pull at one part of it, and if it were to give way, then we risk losing the whole lot. All we have built, good and bad, would break up. And here memories cannot help us. Rather, they would seem to mock us, because they still have not changed. The things that we would hope to return to have long since moved on. Our memories are of things extinguished or frozen partway through.

We can regret memory, and particularly what we did not do. But this must not lead to the calamity of us regretting the present, the palpable reality, and allowing what is long past and long gone to blight what is here now. We need our memories to keep their distance and remain contained. We have to keep them away from us, behind the high wire fence, and it is no one's job to do this but ours.

But what we hope, what we strive for and why we keep our memories contained, is for a happy store. We desire a collection of recollections that can fulfil us, complete us, round us out, make us three-dimensional even as the memories themselves are flat. What we need to do is learn and take on the experience, to use our memories, to examine them and so to examine ourselves. Our memories can help us understand the choices that we have made. But only if we can tame the melancholy of regret and hold onto the reasons for the choices we have made. We may wish that we had taken a different route, but we have to hold off these regrets and instead try to understand why we did what we did, and why we went one way and not another. The reason for this is that, unlike the past, the present remains full of possibility. The present is the place where we still have choices to make, where things are still open to us. And the present is able to place a limit on the speculations, the what-ifs, of memory by reminding us of just what is still here in front of us.

The palpable present helps us to appreciate that the arbitrariness of our decisions – that we could have gone right instead of left – does not make their effects any less concrete. It may have been pure luck that we happened to be in that one place at that precise time that allowed us to meet the love of our life, and it may not have taken much to prevent this meeting. But once it had happened it does become and remain consequential. It cannot be taken back and there then ceases to be anything in the least arbitrary about that action. It now has to be as it is, with all the certainty of that face that is before us and all the shared things we can call on from being together.

This is the very harshness of memory. Even as we are wrapped in sentiment, there is an inexorable pull that does not know how to be gentle, that does not know why we might want to forget some things even as we remember others. Memories leave the judgement to us, but do so without an apparent concern for what implication this may have. The deepening of memory holds onto us and we can do nothing as it grows and grows. And because some of the consequences of our acts and omissions are greater than others, they can cut deeper and sometimes get right to the bone. This is because the finitude there, the very consequentiality of the decision, seems as palpable as the very reality in which we find ourselves. How can we trade the loss of a parent that led to moving continents, for a wife and children found on the other side of the world?[4] How can we trade the real loss – and we can remember the reality of that loss all too well – with the entirely unknown loss that would come from those close to me now never having been with me, or never even existing at all? It is in cases such as this where memory stops being an illusion and becomes seemingly more real than what we wish for in the present. What we are comparing here is a real loss with a hypothetical one. It is precisely that some people are still with us while others are not that causes us the hurt here, even as we find solace in the continued presence of those who are close. But we have lost not them – those still here and close – but someone else, who was once just as real and just as connected to us. So there is a difference in the level of experience here, and this is why memory matters so. This is why memories can both hold us and haunt us; they both tie us and taunt us. Some of what we remember, because of what occurred and to whom, seems to be more real than the reality we have around us.

We can and do live without our loved ones, our parents most commonly. But they never really go away. There is undoubtedly pain involved in the recollection of them. But there is something positive, redemptive even, in the remembering. The thinking of and on memories brings them out and makes them more palpable. This not only

---

4 My father died when I was 8, and we moved back from Australia to the UK, where I have lived ever since and where, 24 years later, I married my wife. We have two daughters, both superbly competent in keeping their father in his place.

brings out the person, but also the place where we find them. We truly cannot separate out the place and the person. So our attempt to capture a person that is still real to us always brings with it a particular place.

Of course, our store of memories is limited and partial. But, no matter how partial, these memories relate strongly to a sense, perhaps even the essence, of a place. One tiny snippet of our past, with no real context, no before or after, can be so very vivid and feel so alive to us. We can feel ourselves there in that place, but we cannot say why and how we are there now in that place that has really become physically very distant. It does seem very arbitrary and uncontrolled. This is where there is always a degree of sadness, and perhaps even a degree of desperation to recapture our being in that place at that time, so that we are again in a position, a physical and emotional relation, where we can say that we *know* these people and this place again.

§

Memories are always located. It may not be that the location is crucial – the memory is not of *it* – but it is always necessary. Memories are always in place and they fit into their space. As such, place is always the context, the canniness of memory, that makes it *heimlich*, homelike, and a comfort to us.

A way of looking at this is to compare these snippets of memory that we find so evocative and emotionally charged with the manner in which we use our dwelling in the present. The routine, quotidian passage through the dwelling, and the manner of our interactions with partner and children or parent, will, we might assume, lead to the formation of those snippets which we and them will call on in 5, 10, 20 years' time. This, as a partner and a parent in particular, places a responsibility on us and could become a source of worry were we to reflect on it, in that we would seek to ensure that we create the right sort of memories, those that are comforting and not harrowing, fondly remembered and not regretted or a source of torment. The worry is that, be it deliberately or as an act of omission, purposefully or in neglect, we will have some negative impact on our partner and children. We might say that we are all the unwitting creators of yearnings in the future, just like the legacy of yearning left by my prematurely deceased father, whom I cannot really remember even as I desperately seek to, and of whom I cannot separate the memory from the stories told by my mother and others who were closer and older, and the photographs I have kept. This responsibility and worry may cause us to freeze, to stop and ponder the consequences of any action we are now considering. But it might, or rather it should, also make us wish to make that relationship as fruitful as possible for as long as it can last. And, of course, we have no real inkling when that ending will come (even as we know it surely will), and so we ought to treat every single occasion as the last.

But there is an obvious problem here, in that these actions are not often, and should not be, reflective. They come, as it were, out of the naturalness of the relationship we have and are the result of other iterated actions and so we cannot see them as strictly deliberative. They are things we just do, which somehow or other stick in the mind and remain available to recall when cued.

The things that we remember – our emotional capital – cannot be collected deliberately. We cannot say that we want any particular event to be the most significant one for us and that we want it to outlive all others. We do not have any direct control over what we remember, on what our unconscious throws back at us. We have no real choice over what we forget and what we remember. There will be much that we appear to forget and that goes unnoticed. But there are other things that we simply cannot ignore and that will not go away. They sneak back into our consciousness and mug us when we least expect them. Often we are not aware of why these snippets return or how it occurs. We do not know why it is significant or why it should be.

What is interesting and welcoming is that as we dwell on these memories they seem to become stronger and clearer. And as we reflect it might be that other memories come back to us that are linked to that person in that place. The spark, as it were, lights a fire of memory and becomes brighter and stronger. We remember more of the place and the people, all of them equally specific and tight in their focus.

I can offer an example here: I have a number of memories from my early childhood that all took place in a room in my grandmother's house. But this is a place that I have literally not seen for 50 years. I now barely remember it and would struggle to describe its individuality, any of the décor or any of the furniture. It does not even look particularly familiar in the many photos my family still have of us in that room. Yet this room appears to be the conduit for many memories, as if they have congregated there in readiness for my returning and once I open the door, once I alight on one of these memories, then others jostle around me clamouring for my attention.

These memories are always specific, such that I do not recollect the whole room. It is only ever just one part of it, the very particular and specific backing to a person who is doing or saying something. This place acts like an aura around the person, as if my memory has cast a spotlight onto the person which only illuminates what is immediately around them. Yet I am also aware of my own presence there, and of that place also holding me, so that I am not looking at things from outside. The room encloses me too and so the light does not just illuminate those I remember, but also, in some way, it illuminates me too.

We can question just how connected we are to places like this that we can recall. In this case, I have no connection to this place and have not had any since my grandmother died in 1967 and the house was sold. I have not been there since and have no certainty over any aspect of this place. My connection is that my father, mother, grandmother and brothers and sister animate this place, and without them it would not matter. I remember it only because of their actions there. This means, of course, that the place is not neutral. It may be passive in being in the background, but it becomes special in memory, in that it is now inseparable from these people and their time, which is also my time. The memory depends on this combination of myself, time, people *and place*. But were I ever asked what the memory is, I would say without hesitation that it is of my father or my mother and not of that place.

Our memories are things that link time, people and place. But also we need a place for our memories. So housing acts as a store of memories, and this operates in two ways. First, it is where we store or keep significant things that resonate with and call to us. But second, as we have just shown, it is the background to those memories themselves, in that these memories are placed, located in this space, which may be a past dwelling. In both cases, however, it is housing that encloses memory.

This does not mean that the dwellings are always necessary for memory. But rather it states that the stability and permanence of our housing, then and now, gives us the ability to recall memories at our leisure *and* the extensive opportunity to create significant moments, relations and connections out of which new memories can be formed. We might suggest that housing, with its privacy and capacity for care-full complacency, offers an opportunity for the benign effects of memory to flourish, both so we can recall them, but also so we can make them.

So just how important is the place to the memory? The events themselves are quite banal and ordinary and are not in any sense place dependent. They were not out of the ordinary or peculiar, and their implications and effects were limited to our family and friends alone. Yet could these things have happened anywhere else? Was not the context important, if only because it provides the enclosure or the frame for these things to occur? These things need not have happened in that place, just as they need not have happened in that way at all. But once they did occur, the event and the place could not be separated and the memory could not then be seen in any other way. This is similar to how we might name a child. Before we choose a name for our newborn daughter she could be called anything. We could be daringly eccentric or boringly traditional. Yet once the child has been named, that is what she becomes and she could not be anything else. That is who she is and it is not in the least arbitrary. The same applies with these memories: they could, in theory, take place anywhere, but not anymore. They did happen in that way and in that place, and now that is all that matters. The significance of the place is not antecedent to the occurrence, but is now intrinsically linked to it. What mattered is that things happened there in that way, and that is the reason we now remember that place. We do not remember it for its amenities, location, décor or space standards, but because we lived and loved there. That for even a short time we animated that space, gave it life and a meaning. It was us, just us, that took that space and breathed into it so that it could enframe our purpose.

Now, looking back, we see this process in another way, as simply framing, as a halo, a dimly remembered casing that has half faded, with no details, only points, small impressions that suggest relations in space for the action to engage in. This is why the space retains some intimacy, because the memory is still in its necessary wrapping even though we might not be able to draw a plan of the house, give an address or take anyone to it. Yet, we can state, that part of our childhood is still there and remains there, because we cannot disassociate the events from the place, and the intimacy from what protects it, even though that space is one into which we can never venture again.

§

We do not experience remembered places in the same manner as we experience the dwelling we live in now, and this is precisely because we can only ever return to the former in memory, whereas with our current dwelling we still haunt the place ourselves along with our remembering. We can still sit in the same place we were when we watched our children take their first steps. Our children may have now grown and we may hanker for those past times and regret their passing. But we can still view this place differently, as a place of possibility, and this is because we are still using it, and because we can still use it so we can create new meanings. We might be less inclined to dwell on the past simply because in our current place we can still conceive of new things happening. Where we are now remains as a place of imagining as well as memory. The space is not just linked to memory but also to possibility, to the opportunity for new memory formation, which will, in turn, be linked to this place. This continued possibility means that we can see the dwelling differently, such that we can take it for granted and dwell on it less than one we can no longer touch.

Yet this is precisely how we always live and always have done. It is how we lived in those places now gone. We do not treat our dwelling as a shrine until we have lost it. We accept that the dwelling will change as our use for it changes and the relations within the dwelling alter. It is only in hindsight, once the dwelling is lost to us, that we see it differently, and so we seek to remember those significant moments and find they come with a place attached.

While we can agree with Gaston Bachelard, who wrote in his *The Poetics of Space*[5] that the house is necessary for daydreaming, we also need to remember that a house is also necessary for memory formation, that unless we have a place, much of the fondness, joy and closeness that forms our memories is impossible. Instead we have nightmare, a sense of the uncanny, the German *unheimlich* being especially pertinent here. The comfort we take from memory shows the resilience of the *heimlich*, that dwelling is carried by memory to reinforce our homely sense. Our memories, so to speak, are pleasantly located and well furnished.

§

These remembered but distant places still have their uses for us, even as we have lost them as physical places that we can visit and animate. But that being so, can we still claim that we are intimate with a place that we can no longer visit, and indeed may not have been near for 50 years? Can we still suggest that this place is in any way ours?

Of course we cannot in any legal sense. But it is still ours in memory, even as we have to accept that the place has ossified, that it has in a way died, in that it does not and cannot develop. The place is now stuck in that one time when it meant something for us and is part of a very specific set of memories. We appreciate that the place will have changed. If it still exists, it will now be owned and dwelt in by others who will have changed it and who have formed their own associations with it after us. We only then really possess the memory of the place as it was in that point in time we had direct contact with it. We

5 Bachelard (1969).

may hold onto these images with great fondness and refer to them as ours, but it is no longer the same as the real place. It has become a different place.

What may very well help us to maintain the illusion of it being ours is precisely that we make no attempt to see or visit it again. To see others using it, to see how it has been altered from our remembering, would disabuse us and potentially despoil the memory of the place as it was. Perhaps this is important precisely because we do not remember the place for itself, but rather for it being the frame or the background for other events. We see ourselves in it, we recall what happened there, but what is going on there now does not matter and would unnecessarily complicate the picture for us. And, in any case, it is not the place that we wish to own, but what was within it. It is the contents of that place that we insist to be well and truly ours. To do anything more than this would be to, so to speak, foreground the place and to superimpose it over the memories themselves. It would be as if the actions we wish to focus on fade as the colours in the background brighten and come alive. We do not want, therefore, to have a new stage or to have it refurbished; we do not want to be forced to take notice of it any more than when it has our very own particular shadow cast upon it.

So, we might suggest, we feel we own it provided we leave it exactly as it is, that we do not seek to renew our acquaintance in any other way but through memory, and that we do not seek it out as a physical space. If we leave it alone we are free to imagine it as we want it to be still, in all its inexactitude and vagueness perhaps, but as an attachment, as the frame for those significant shards of memory.

Chapter 6
What housing does

Housing is hard to understand. It loses any shape when it is observed too closely and becomes a symbol, an emblem for something else, a cipher for our ambitions and aspirations. The flow of housing stops when we notice it. It depends on unconscious activity, on movement apparently only for its own sake. Housing is only so important to us because we are able to ignore it and get on with other things.

Perhaps we ought to admit that housing has to be felt rather than defined. We have to absorb it while it absorbs us. We come to know housing – as *our* housing – only by proximity and engagement, by the truth of our combination. Housing needs no mediation. It is just housing and ourselves, with no intermediary. We have to become a part of it, while it becomes part of us. Housing is meaningful, but only for so long as we do not reflect on its meaning. To see housing is to risk losing sight of it. We might become too conscious of it; or worse, we might seek merely to preserve it.

So what housing does might be better left unsaid. The saying, once said, is no longer housing, but a distorted reflection, an approximation, of what housing does. The saying takes us out of housing and into a different type of space. So there is always artificiality in thinking on housing, and this is due to the mechanics of thinking and not the nature of housing. Thinking is always distinct from housing, even as it is *on* housing. But we can have thinking that gets us nearer to housing once we recognise – through thinking – what housing does. Our thinking is a flow of understanding that can take us nearer to housing.

So we should think on housing. But, in doing so, we have to recognise that to think on housing is to stop using it. Housing ceases to be subject to us and instead it becomes an object. In this way, thinking about housing is a potentially dangerous and self-destructive passion. We prevent housing from doing what it does as we stand and watch it. It is indeed fortunate that very few see the need for their thinking.

Reflecting on housing can also be a mirror that presents a distorted image of ourselves. But this is only because our reflecting is misplaced. We are looking for the wrong things in the wrong way. We are guilty of relying on a distorted vision. We are searching to create significance *outside* of housing. We are trying to find patterns that allow us to embed housing and to quantify it.

In reflecting we forget that it is the banality of housing that saves us from delving too deeply into it, and so we can get on with our lives. Finding patterns in housing is the sign that you should stop looking. There is no pattern, there is nothing generalisable that does not stop us from using housing as we should.

But housing is not always silent. It can speak, and it knows more than we ever can. Housing can tell us things, but only if we know how to ask. We have to be able to think about housing in the proper manner. And we have to know with what language housing speaks.

What aids us is that there is an essential sameness to housing, even as it appears different and even as its uniqueness is what defines it as housing we can use. We might say that housing is culturally determined in the same way that language is. It appears different from place to place, but the process and purpose remains the same. Housing communicates to us in the same way even as the language is different. But it can only speak to us when we use it.

§

We have sought to express what housing does and so have been careful to reclaim housing from those who only see the façade. But, in doing so, housing has not become a different object. Our focus has been on the meanings that we attach to this object, an act which then allows us to use its implacability to forget or ignore the object's physicality.

Housing is near and far, open and closed. It is embedded in our memories and our memories are embedded in it. Housing forms the frame in which we see others and behind which they might choose to hide. But it is also the place to which we can always return; even if is only to mourn.

Housing is the enclosure of care-full complacency. Care is the complacent continuing on within housing enabled by implacability and benign indifference. Care and enclosure link us to housing as a physical object, and they tell us why we need to be dry, warm and free from predation. But this is not all. Through the implacability of housing our care is unimpeded and we are able to remain close. The implacability of enclosure allows for privacy. But it also lets us focus on care and so ignore the threat of aggregation that comes in order to enhance aspiration. Housing stands implacably, enabling use and demanding indifference through the hardness of its face. Housing yields through use, as internal pressure, but without bowing to the external. Housing lets us be useful through our care.

Aspiration turns housing from care into competition. It forces value onto housing and makes it contingent. Aspiration is where we use housing to be elsewhere.

Policy is made for aspiration, but it can do so only through aggregation and the standardisation of housing. Policy sees only the façade of housing and places an extrinsic value on the exclusivity of the implacable.

To understand what housing does we must think properly and place housing in the context of care-full use and not extrinsic value. Housing is an expression of the need for care and is able to then maintain care by its implacability towards the external.

Housing is both a noun and a verb. It is a thing and an activity. What brings these together is meaningful use. Use mixes the thing with our care. We know housing heals, but it can also fail. It can be a sponsor of aspiration and motive. It is not an unalloyed good but a thing of ordinary use. Housing is as fallen as we are.

Housing allows us to speak generally and without prescription. We are not saying we must live according to one pattern or another, merely that we can have a pattern built by *our* connection to *our* housing. A focus on use means we can say why housing works, and why it does not. We do not sentimentalise housing as 'homes', but nor do we seek perfection in our daily chores.

So what does housing do? It allows us to continue.

A note on sources

Academics are meant to show their sources, and there is a clear and good purpose in doing this. We need to show where our ideas and arguments have come from. This is not just so we can show that we are not plagiarising or misusing the work of others, but also to make apparent the connections with the broader academic and intellectual community. Yet, several of the essays in this book have been presented directly and without direct reference to any sources, and others are only lightly referenced.

This was done only after a lot of thought and only after seeking the advice of several people whose views I respect. It became clear to me that this approach suited the style and speculative approach of the project. Of course, my ideas and thoughts have not come out of nowhere, and I have many intellectual debts to acknowledge. However, rather than clog up the text with a great many footnotes or references, I have chosen to detail them here.

There are two further reasons for doing this. First, a good many of the sources I have used are my own previous works. Several of the essays presented here are essentially attempts to bring together ideas on housing and dwelling from a number of my works with the aim of creating a cohesive, if rather condensed, whole. Of course, I used many sources in writing these initial works, which are all conventional in terms of length and scholarly apparatus. The original sources can be found in the respective bibliographies, and so it would be redundant to reproduce them here (and this also explains why the bibliography below is rather brief).

Second, these essays have been influenced by a number of thinkers without making direct reference to them. John Turner has been an enduring influence, particularly on my ideas regarding policy. Both Gaston Bachelard and Martin Heidegger have deeply affected my views on dwelling and the subjective use of housing. A more recent influence is Emanuel Swedenborg and his doctrine of use. This is rather more indirect, but it has certainly had an impact on the discussions of use and aspiration.

While the Preface serves mainly as a justification for this work, it does link to two of my earlier works, *The Limits of Housing Policy* (1996), which was a much altered version of my PhD thesis, and *The Social Philosophy of Housing* (2003), although some of my thinking on a philosophical approach to housing has shifted away to some extent from the latter work.

There are two main sources for the essay 'Thinking on housing', both of which are my own works. First, in *The Limits of Housing Policy* (1996), I critique the nature of housing policy and how it differs from housing. Second, in my paper 'Using Theory or Making Theory: Can There Be Theories of Housing?' (King, 2009) I look at whether we can consider housing conceptually and argue that we should seek to build concepts and theories from within housing. I should add that a key influence on my early ideas on housing and particularly on *The Limits of Housing Policy* was John Turner's *Housing by People* (1976). This is a book I have read literally a dozen times, and it was the inspiration for wanting to write philosophically on housing. The main source for the brief discussion on the speculative approach to philosophy is Dylan Moran's *Introduction to Phenomenology* (2000).

The key source for the essay 'Housing is' is Enrique Enriquez's *Tarology* (2011), which identifies his playful approach and backs this up with some discussion on the language of the birds and pataphysics. Enriquez's later book *Linguistick* (2013) takes the deconstruction of words even further. As stated in the notes for the essay, there is also a film of Enriquez at work, titled (like his earlier book) *Tarology* (2013; directed by Chris Deleo). For a discussion on pataphysics the best starting point is Andrew Hughill's *Pataphysics: A Useless Guide* (2012), the title of which nicely displays the nature of the subject.

The essay 'Care-full use' essentially brings together my ideas on the nature of housing in a highly condensed form. It is based largely on my works on dwelling and our use of housing, namely *Private Dwelling* (2004), *The Common Place* (2005) and *In Dwelling* (2008). These books used an introspective method to analyse housing from the inside. What I have done in 'Care-full use' is to take out the anecdotes and examples and try to present an abstract distillation of the nature of housing as an object of use. In addition, it will be clear that I owe a debt to Gaston Bachelard (1969) and Martin Heidegger (1962, 1993) for the phenomenological approach taken up in this piece. For the avoidance of any ambiguity, however, my use of the concept of care is rather different from that of Heidegger in *Being and Time*. I should also acknowledge Stanley Rosen and his work *The Elusiveness of the Ordinary* (2002) as a key influence in forming these ideas. As stated above, this essay is imbued with Emanuel Swedenborg's ideas of useful service. Swedenborg discusses the idea of use and useful service throughout his works, but the best starting point is *The Divine Love and Wisdom* (1987).

Likewise, the essay 'Misuse' is based on my earlier work and also presents these ideas in a much condensed form. The discussion on policy relies on the aforementioned *The Limits of Housing Policy*. The comments on aspiration have developed out of earlier thoughts that can be found in *Housing Boom and Bust* (King, 2010). These ideas also link to work undertaken as part of my book *The Antimodern Condition* (King, 2014), where I looked at the materialistic nature of modernity.

The penultimate essay, 'The consequences of use', points to the two important sources at the start of the piece, namely Mikhail Bakhtin (1981) and Emile Cioran (1995). These writers provide ideas that I use to go off on a range of tangents. Gaston Bachelard (1969) was again important in framing my ideas on memory, as were Roland Barthes' *Camera Lucida* (1993) and Jacques Derrida's *The Work of Mourning* (2001). For an interesting philosophical discussion on framing and its significance, see Stephen Mulhall's *On Film* (2002). This essay also links to my earlier books *Private Dwelling* and *In Dwelling*, where I explore the subjectivity of our use of housing.

Bachelard, G. (1969): *The Poetics of Space*, Boston, Beacon.
Bakhtin, M. (1981): *The Dialogic Imagination: Four Essays*, Austin, University of Texas Press.
Barthes, R. (1993): *Camera Lucida: Reflections on Photography*, London, Vintage.
Cioran, E. M. (1995): *Tears and Saints*, Chicago, Chicago University Press.
Derrida, J. (2001): *The Work of Mourning*, Chicago, Chicago University Press.
Enriquez, E. (2011): *Tarology*, Roskilde, EyeCorner Press.
Enriquez, E. (2013): *Linguistick*, Roskilde, EyeCorner Press.
Heidegger, M. (1962): *Being and Time*, Oxford, Blackwell.
Heidegger, M. (1993): *Basic Writings*, revised and expanded edition, London, Routledge.
Hughill, A. (2012): *Pataphysics: A Useless Guide*, Cambridge, MA, MIT Press.
King, P. (1996): *The Limits of Housing Policy: A Philosophical Investigation*, London, Middlesex University Press.
King, P. (2003): *A Social Philosophy of Housing*, Aldershot, Ashgate.

King, P. (2004): *Private Dwelling: Contemplating the Use of Housing*, London, Routledge.

King, P. (2005): *The Common Place: The Ordinary Experience of Housing*, Aldershot, Ashgate.

King, P. (2008): *In Dwelling: Implacability, Exclusion and Acceptance*, Aldershot, Ashgate.

King, P. (2009): 'Using Theory or Making Theory: Can There Be Theories of Housing?', *Housing, Theory and Society*, 26:1, pp. 41–52.

King, P. (2010): *Housing Boom and Bust: Owner Occupation, Government Regulation and the Credit Crunch*, London, Routledge.

King, P. (2014): *The Antimodern Condition: An Argument against Progress*, Farnham, Ashgate.

Moran, D. (2000): *Introduction to Phenomenology*, London, Routledge.

Mulhall, S. (2002): *On Film*, London, Routledge.

Rosen, S. (2002): *The Elusiveness of the Ordinary: Studies in the Possibility of Philosophy*, New Haven, Yale University Press.

Swedenborg, E. (1987): *The Divine Love and Wisdom*, London, The Swedenborg Society.

Turner, J. (1976): *Housing by People: Towards Autonomy in Building Environments*, London, Marion Boyars.

Index